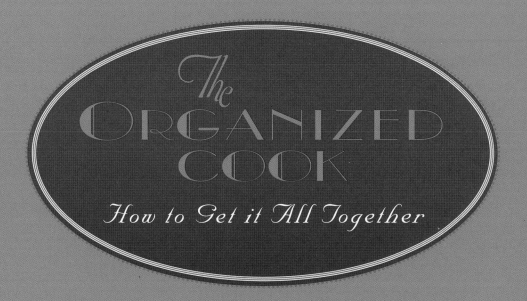

The
ORGANIZED
COOK

How to Get it All Together

J U D Y   B U S C H

Illustrations by Carolyn Bucha

bright sky press

Albany, Texas • New York, New York

Acknowledgments

Thanks:

To my agent Elaine Markson for saying yes, it could be done; to Kate Hartson, gentle editor; to Carolyn Bucha for painting life into the words; and to Carol Jessop who made the book just sit up and sing.

To dear friends and family for all of the times we've broken bread together—or talked about it over hundreds, sometimes thousands of miles—and who, by their very beings, insist that the cooking is only a part of the conversation: to my sister Wendy Connell who is always there; to Lilian Cooksey and all of the warmth she engenders in that stone barn house including her memorized passages of Elizabeth David; to Peggy Hosbach, dear pal, for the wonderful thousands of hours together; to Pat Kramer whose fierce generosity never stops; to Catherine Lorraine from the time she was seventeen and drowning us in garlic until now—every one of those conversations; to Elaine Markson—again—because she makes it all look so easy.

To Nick and Ben and Tracy for being exactly who they are, with love.

And, of course, to Fred who has said it was all wonderful from the first taste of the first tuna casserole.

Fred, of course . . . .

b

bright sky press

Albany, Texas
New York, New York

Text copyright © 2002 by Judith Busch
Illustrations copyright © 2002 by Carolyn Bucha

Library of Congress Cataloging-in-Publication Data

Busch, Judy, 1941 –
    The organized cook / Judy Busch
    p. cm.
    ISBN 0-9709987-2-4 (alk. paper)
    1. Entertaining. 2. Cookery. I. Title.
    TX731 .B84 2002
    642'.4—dc21

                                    2001052848

Book and cover design by Carol Jessop, Black Trout Design
Illustrations by Carolyn Bucha
Printed in China by Asia Pacific Offset

INTRODUCTION

Cooking for friends and family is one of the great pleasures on this earth. From the anticipation we have about the good company, the planning of the meal and the discussion of what we will cook and, my husband's favorite, what wine and beverages we will serve, to the shopping, preparing and, finally, the serving of the meal, there is a singular kind of enjoyment and well-being that comes from the whole process.

Of course, that is when things are going well. But—ah, that treacherous word—we do not always have the luxury of a leisurely development of a meal. Yet, the guests are invited and the meal must be prepared. Those are the times when a foundation of strong organization comes in and when this workbook for organizing your cooking and entertaining life enters.

My husband and I have cooked countless meals for guests. Sometimes we have the luxury of cooking over several days or on leisurely Saturdays in anticipation of the happy evenings we will spend with friends. Sometimes— all too often—the meal is prepared on a weeknight after a challenging day at work. And, frequently, there are guests for a weekend or longer.

Over the years, in organizing these meals, I have made lists of what had to be done—food and wine purchased, table set, steps taken to prepare the meal, times when food had to go into the oven and come out. As you know even if you've had guests for a meal only once in your life, the key to entertaining successfully is organization. There is some subtle psychology in the fact that, when the hosts are organized and at ease, when they are clearly in charge of an occasion, the guests are more comfortable. Few of us have escaped being guests of a worried host and, therefore, players in an edgy evening, each guest nervous on behalf of the host. Alas, few of us have escaped being that worried host. Sometimes this awkwardness is simply inexperience and is understandable. For those with more experience, the awkward evening generally results from a lack of organization. There are scores of reasons for this and I've been victim of most of them. Sometimes I'm too rushed. Sometimes the guests, for one reason or another, are asked at the last minute and I've not had a chance to prepare adequately. Sometimes I've been too busy and simply have not had the time to think about entertaining.

It is true that there are some who are natural hosts, rare people who breeze smoothly from work to dinner party, the evening's entertaining a sort of intricate mental chess game they play, knowing all the while that they will win. These people greet their guests with the ease of someone who has just gone for a quiet stroll on the first fair day of spring.

But I am not one of them. And I've had to compensate for the lack of internal sense of structure with methods of external organization— simple, unencumbering ways to organize graceful meals to share with friends and relations. Over the years, a few simple forms emerged that allow me to know what foods we have on hand, what foods we like and are easy to make, what we are going to serve for a specific meal and, finally, how the table will look for that meal— the elements of easy and successful entertaining.

This may sound like a lot of paper work. It is not. These elements flow together naturally and easily. You add to them as your inclination and schedule permit. They are personal and particular to you and your style.

If you are one of those rare animals for whom preparing for guests is as natural as strolling down a country lane, you may not need this assistance. This book is for the rest of us for whom the music is not quite so inherent, but who enjoy cooking and entertaining and wish the process were simpler and more pleasant.

GUESTS FOR A MEAL

*I*n my mind, the perfect meal is a "simple little meal." The very words conjure up a meal that is fresh and easy, a meal which has a certain spontaneity to it, a meal which is uncluttered by artifice, a meal which honors our guests and puts them at ease.

Now, the very words "simple little meal" are, as anyone who has made one can tell you, a euphemism. The simplicity is in the eye—and mouth and mind—of the beholder. A meal may be simple to the guest who sits down to a perfect dinner for early spring —say grilled lamb kebobs in a mustard marinade, roasted asparagus, steamed new potatoes with parsley, a salad of spring greens with a curl of good Parmesan, a sourdough baguette, and, for dessert, a strawberry tart. A flinty *Sancerre* or robust young *Côtes du Rhône* could accompany this meal. You can even see the table. There might be daffodils in a spongewear bowl sitting atop a delicately hued Provençal scarf. There will be candles if it's evening. And it will be a "simple little meal."

Except that someone has to make that meal and that someone is YOU. Even with the least amount of preparation, someone has to shop for the groceries, wash and cut the vegetables, make the marinade and prepare the meat, set up the grill, make the tart shell and probably the crème which forms the bed for the strawberries, wash and hull the berries. Someone has to pick or buy the daffodils and figure out that the spongewear bowl (which will need washing since it's been on the shelf for a while) and the Provençal scarf are right for the moment. So by the time the guests arrive for the simple little meal, you could be a profoundly tired host unless you're able to put some of this work on automatic pilot.

Somewhere in the middle of preparing innumerable "simple little meals," with my pen poised on the list I made to get organized, my hand hovering to check off "coffee" and move on to "cream," it dawned on me—dawn is sometimes exceedingly slow to arrive—that this list and I had been trafficking together for a long time with neither of us the wiser for the experience. I realized that I had made this same list each and every time we had guests for a meal. I had used valuable brain cells remembering, each time, the parts of the meal—the crucial tiny attentions that contribute to the whole.

So at that very moment—probably not as rushed as usual—I sat down at the computer and made The List once and for all. I called it "Guests for a Meal"—I sought serviceability, not a song title—and cranked out a few copies. Then I happily proceeded to invite friends and relations to lunch and to dinner, confident now that I was saving energy for the larger endeavors—cooking and visiting with guests.

On the following pages are Guests for a Meal forms. Plan your meal using the form. As you do, you will easily see what you have prepared for the meal and what you have left to do. You will be able to arrange the time schedule of each part of the meal so that a logical sequence of tasks is written down. (Of course, you will also do in advance as much as possible.) And, when your guests arrive, you will be able to relax and enjoy their company rather than worry about remembering what you need to do next.

There is a certain reassurance in knowing that something is written down, in not having to think, say, about the strawberries because there they are right on the page, that you will not forget to grind the coffee beans nor pour the cream nor cut the flowers nor put the asparagus into the oven at how many degrees. The timing out, the organizational thinking is already done for you and you are free to try to remember where the Provençal scarf actually is or to wonder if the mint has grown enough so you can put a few leaves on the tart.

And, besides, the rule goes, once on paper, always on paper. I've provided thirty pages of Guests for a Meal forms in this book so that you can keep a permanent record and can flip through as I do to see what meals (some great, some a little more pedestrian, what with the after-work dash) you've had, and with whom. After all, repeating great meals (simple little ones or not) is a remarkably efficient and smart idea, but repeating them with the same people is not very bright at all.

Guests for a Meal

Date: _____

Guests: _____   _____

_____   _____

_____   _____

_____   _____

_____

Hors d'Oeuvres: _____

First Course: _____

Main Course: _____

Vegetable(s): _____

Starch: _____

Salad and Salad Dressing: _____

Bread: _____

Dessert: _____

Wine or Beverage: _____

☐ Coffee ☐ Cream ☐ Sugar ☐ Coffee Cups

☐ Bar:

_____

☐ Ice ☐ Glasses

☐ Set table:

_____

☐ Flowers:

☐ Starters—napkins, forks

☐ After dinner:

_____

☐ Other:

_____

Guests for a Meal
Schedule

Week before: _____
_____
_____
_____
_____
_____

Day before: _____
_____
_____
_____
_____

Day of meal:	task	time

Guests for a Meal

Date: _____

Guests: _____   _____

_____   _____

_____   _____

_____   _____

_____   _____

Hors d'Oeuvres: _____

First Course: _____

Main Course: _____

Vegetable(s): _____

Starch: _____

Salad and Salad Dressing: _____

Bread: _____

Dessert: _____

Wine or Beverage: _____

❏ Coffee ❏ Cream ❏ Sugar ❏ Coffee Cups

❏ Bar:

_____

❏ Ice ❏ Glasses

❏ Set table:

_____

❏ Flowers:

❏ Starters—napkins, forks

❏ After dinner:

_____

❏ Other:

_____

Guests for a Meal
Schedule

Week before: _____
_____
_____
_____
_____

Day before: _____
_____
_____
_____
_____

Day of meal: task   time
_____   _____
_____   _____
_____   _____
_____   _____
_____   _____
_____   _____
_____   _____

Guests for a Meal

Date: _____

Guests: _____   _____

        _____   _____

        _____   _____

        _____   _____

        _____   _____

Hors d'Oeuvres: _____

First Course: _____

Main Course: _____

Vegetable(s): _____

Starch: _____

Salad and Salad Dressing: _____

Bread: _____

Dessert: _____

Wine or Beverage: _____

☐ Coffee   ☐ Cream   ☐ Sugar   ☐ Coffee Cups

☐ Bar:

_____

☐ Ice   ☐ Glasses

☐ Set table:

_____

☐ Flowers:

☐ Starters—napkins, forks

☐ After dinner:

_____

☐ Other:

_____

Guests for a Meal
Schedule

Week before: _____
_____
_____
_____
_____
_____

Day before: _____
_____
_____
_____
_____

Day of meal: task   time
_____
_____
_____
_____
_____
_____
_____
_____
_____

Guests for a Meal

Date: _____

Guests: _____   _____

_____   _____

_____   _____

_____   _____

_____   _____

Hors d'Oeuvres: _____

First Course: _____

Main Course: _____

Vegetable(s): _____

Starch: _____

Salad and Salad Dressing: _____

Bread: _____

Dessert: _____

Wine or Beverage: _____

☐ Coffee ☐ Cream ☐ Sugar ☐ Coffee Cups

☐ Bar:

_____

☐ Ice ☐ Glasses

☐ Set table:

_____

☐ Flowers:

☐ Starters—napkins, forks

☐ After dinner:

_____

☐ Other:

_____

Guests for a Meal
Schedule

Week before: _____
_____
_____
_____
_____
_____

Day before: _____
_____
_____
_____
_____
_____

Day of meal: task   time
_____   _____
_____   _____
_____   _____
_____   _____
_____   _____
              _____   _____
              _____   _____
              _____   _____
              _____   _____
              _____   _____

Guests for a Meal

Date: _____

Guests: _____   _____

_____   _____

_____   _____

_____   _____

_____   _____

Hors d'Oeuvres: _____

First Course: _____

Main Course: _____

Vegetable(s): _____

Starch: _____

Salad and Salad Dressing: _____

Bread: _____

Dessert: _____

Wine or Beverage: _____

☐ Coffee   ☐ Cream   ☐ Sugar   ☐ Coffee Cups

☐ Bar:

_____

☐ Ice   ☐ Glasses

☐ Set table:

_____

☐ Flowers:

☐ Starters—napkins, forks

☐ After dinner:

_____

☐ Other:

_____

Guests for a Meal
Schedule

Week before: _____
_____
_____
_____
_____
_____

Day before: _____
_____
_____
_____
_____

Day of meal: task   time
_____   _____
_____   _____
_____   _____
_____   _____
          _____   _____
          _____   _____
          _____   _____
          _____   _____

Guests for a Meal

Date: _____

Guests: _____   _____

             _____   _____

             _____   _____

             _____   _____

             _____   _____

Hors d'Oeuvres: _____

First Course: _____

Main Course: _____

Vegetable(s): _____

Starch: _____

Salad and Salad Dressing: _____

Bread: _____

Dessert: _____

Wine or Beverage: _____

❑ Coffee ❑ Cream ❑ Sugar ❑ Coffee Cups

❑ Bar:

_____

❑ Ice ❑ Glasses

❑ Set table:

_____

❑ Flowers:

❑ Starters—napkins, forks

❑ After dinner:

_____

❑ Other:

_____

Guests for a Meal
Schedule

Week before: _____
_____
_____
_____
_____
_____

Day before: _____
_____
_____
_____
_____

Day of meal: task   time

_____   _____
_____   _____
_____   _____
_____   _____
_____   _____
_____   _____
_____   _____
_____   _____
_____   _____

Guests for a Meal

Date: _____

Guests: _____   _____

_____   _____

_____   _____

_____   _____

_____   _____

Hors d'Oeuvres: _____

First Course: _____

Main Course: _____

Vegetable(s): _____

Starch: _____

Salad and Salad Dressing: _____

Bread: _____

Dessert: _____

Wine or Beverage: _____

❑ Coffee ❑ Cream ❑ Sugar ❑ Coffee Cups

❑ Bar: _____

_____

❑ Ice ❑ Glasses

❑ Set table: _____

_____

❑ Flowers: _____

❑ Starters—napkins, forks

❑ After dinner: _____

_____

❑ Other: _____

_____

Guests for a Meal
Schedule

Week before: _____
_____
_____
_____
_____
_____

Day before: _____
_____
_____
_____
_____

Day of meal: task   time
_____   _____
_____   _____
_____   _____
_____   _____
_____   _____
_____   _____
_____   _____
_____   _____

Guests for a Meal

Date: _____

Guests: _____   _____

_____   _____

_____   _____

_____   _____

_____   _____

Hors d'Oeuvres: _____

First Course: _____

Main Course: _____

Vegetable(s): _____

Starch: _____

Salad and Salad Dressing: _____

Bread: _____

Dessert: _____

Wine or Beverage: _____

☐ Coffee ☐ Cream ☐ Sugar ☐ Coffee Cups

☐ Bar:

_____

☐ Ice ☐ Glasses

☐ Set table:

_____

☐ Flowers:

☐ Starters—napkins, forks

☐ After dinner:

_____

☐ Other:

_____

Guests for a Meal
Schedule

Week before: _____
_____
_____
_____
_____
_____

Day before: _____
_____
_____
_____
_____

Day of meal:	task	time
_____	_____	_____
_____	_____	_____
_____	_____	_____
_____	_____	_____
_____	_____	_____
_____	_____	_____
_____	_____	_____
_____	_____	_____
_____	_____	_____

Guests for a Meal

Date: _____

Guests: _____   _____

_____   _____

_____   _____

_____   _____

_____   _____

Hors d'Oeuvres: _____

First Course: _____

Main Course: _____

Vegetable(s): _____

Starch: _____

Salad and Salad Dressing: _____

Bread: _____

Dessert: _____

Wine or Beverage: _____

☐ Coffee ☐ Cream ☐ Sugar ☐ Coffee Cups

☐ Bar:

_____

☐ Ice ☐ Glasses

☐ Set table:

_____

☐ Flowers:

☐ Starters—napkins, forks

☐ After dinner:

_____

☐ Other:

_____

Guests for a Meal
Schedule

Week before: _____
_____
_____
_____
_____

Day before: _____
_____
_____
_____
_____

Day of meal: task   time
_____   _____
_____   _____
_____   _____
_____   _____
_____   _____
     _____   _____
     _____   _____
          _____   _____
               _____   _____
               _____   _____

Guests for a Meal

Date: _____

Guests: _____   _____

_____   _____

_____   _____

_____   _____

_____   _____

Hors d'Oeuvres: _____

First Course: _____

Main Course: _____

Vegetable(s): _____

Starch: _____

Salad and Salad Dressing: _____

Bread: _____

Dessert: _____

Wine or Beverage: _____

❑ Coffee   ❑ Cream   ❑ Sugar   ❑ Coffee Cups

❑ Bar:

_____

❑ Ice   ❑ Glasses

❑ Set table:

_____

❑ Flowers:

❑ Starters—napkins, forks

❑ After dinner:

_____

❑ Other:

_____

Guests for a Meal
Schedule

Week before: _____

_____

_____

_____

_____

Day before: _____

_____

_____

_____

_____

Day of meal: task   time

_____   _____

_____   _____

_____   _____

_____   _____

_____   _____

_____   _____

_____   _____

_____   _____

_____   _____

Guests for a Meal

Date: _____

Guests: _____   _____

_____   _____

_____   _____

_____   _____

_____   _____

Hors d'Oeuvres: _____

First Course: _____

Main Course: _____

Vegetable(s): _____

Starch: _____

Salad and Salad Dressing: _____

Bread: _____

Dessert: _____

Wine or Beverage: _____

❏ Coffee   ❏ Cream   ❏ Sugar   ❏ Coffee Cups

❏ Bar:

_____

❏ Ice   ❏ Glasses

❏ Set table:

_____

❏ Flowers:

❏ Starters—napkins, forks

❏ After dinner:

_____

❏ Other:

_____

Guests for a Meal
Schedule

Week before: _____
_____
_____
_____
_____

Day before: _____
_____
_____
_____
_____

Day of meal: task   time
_____   _____
_____   _____
_____   _____
_____   _____
        _____   _____
            _____   _____
                _____   _____
                    _____   _____
                        _____   _____

Guests for a Meal

Date: _____

Guests: _____   _____

_____   _____

_____   _____

_____   _____

_____   _____

Hors d'Oeuvres: _____

First Course: _____

Main Course: _____

Vegetable(s): _____

Starch: _____

Salad and Salad Dressing: _____

Bread: _____

Dessert: _____

Wine or Beverage: _____

☐ Coffee ☐ Cream ☐ Sugar ☐ Coffee Cups

☐ Bar:

_____

☐ Ice ☐ Glasses

☐ Set table:

_____

☐ Flowers:

☐ Starters—napkins, forks

☐ After dinner:

_____

☐ Other:

_____

Guests for a Meal
Schedule

Week before: _____
_____
_____
_____
_____
_____

Day before: _____
_____
_____
_____
_____
_____

Day of meal: task   time
_____   _____
_____   _____
_____   _____
_____   _____
_____   _____
_____   _____
_____   _____
_____   _____
_____   _____

Guests for a Meal

Date: _____

Guests: _____   _____

                 _____   _____

                 _____   _____

                 _____   _____

                 _____   _____

Hors d'Oeuvres: _____

First Course: _____

Main Course: _____

Vegetable(s): _____

Starch: _____

Salad and Salad Dressing: _____

Bread: _____

Dessert: _____

Wine or Beverage: _____

☐ Coffee   ☐ Cream   ☐ Sugar   ☐ Coffee Cups

☐ Bar:

_____

☐ Ice   ☐ Glasses

☐ Set table:

_____

☐ Flowers:

☐ Starters—napkins, forks

☐ After dinner:

_____

☐ Other:

_____

Guests for a Meal

Schedule

Week before: _____

_____

_____

_____

_____

Day before: _____

_____

_____

_____

_____

Day of meal: task   time

_____   _____

_____   _____

_____   _____

_____   _____

_____   _____

_____   _____

_____   _____

_____   _____

_____   _____

Guests for a Meal

Date: _____

Guests: _____   _____

_____   _____

_____   _____

_____   _____

_____   _____

Hors d'Oeuvres: _____

First Course: _____

Main Course: _____

Vegetable(s): _____

Starch: _____

Salad and Salad Dressing: _____

Bread: _____

Dessert: _____

Wine or Beverage: _____

☐ Coffee   ☐ Cream   ☐ Sugar   ☐ Coffee Cups

☐ Bar:

_____

☐ Ice   ☐ Glasses

☐ Set table:

_____

☐ Flowers:

☐ Starters—napkins, forks

☐ After dinner:

_____

☐ Other:

_____

Guests for a Meal

Schedule

Week before: _____

_____

_____

_____

_____

Day before: _____

_____

_____

_____

_____

Day of meal: task   time

_____   _____

_____   _____

_____   _____

_____   _____

_____   _____

_____   _____

_____   _____

_____   _____

Guests for a Meal

Date: _____

Guests: _____   _____

_____   _____

_____   _____

_____   _____

_____   _____

Hors d'Oeuvres: _____

First Course: _____

Main Course: _____

Vegetable(s): _____

Starch: _____

Salad and Salad Dressing: _____

Bread: _____

Dessert: _____

Wine or Beverage: _____

☐ Coffee ☐ Cream ☐ Sugar ☐ Coffee Cups

☐ Bar:

_____

☐ Ice ☐ Glasses

☐ Set table:

_____

☐ Flowers:

☐ Starters—napkins, forks

☐ After dinner:

_____

☐ Other:

_____

Guests for a Meal
Schedule

Week before: _____

_____

_____

_____

_____

_____

Day before: _____

_____

_____

_____

_____

_____

Day of meal: task   time

_____   _____

_____   _____

_____   _____

_____   _____

_____   _____

_____   _____

        _____   _____

        _____   _____

        _____   _____

        _____   _____

Guests for a Meal

Date: _____

Guests: _____   _____

_____   _____

_____   _____

_____   _____

_____   _____

Hors d'Oeuvres: _____

First Course: _____

Main Course: _____

Vegetable(s): _____

Starch: _____

Salad and Salad Dressing: _____

Bread: _____

Dessert: _____

Wine or Beverage: _____

❑ Coffee ❑ Cream ❑ Sugar ❑ Coffee Cups

❑ Bar:

_____

❑ Ice ❑ Glasses

❑ Set table:

_____

❑ Flowers:

❑ Starters—napkins, forks

❑ After dinner:

_____

❑ Other:

_____

Guests for a Meal

Schedule

Week before: _____
_____
_____
_____
_____
_____

Day before: _____
_____
_____
_____
_____

Day of meal: task   time
_____
_____
_____
_____
_____
_____
_____
_____
_____
_____

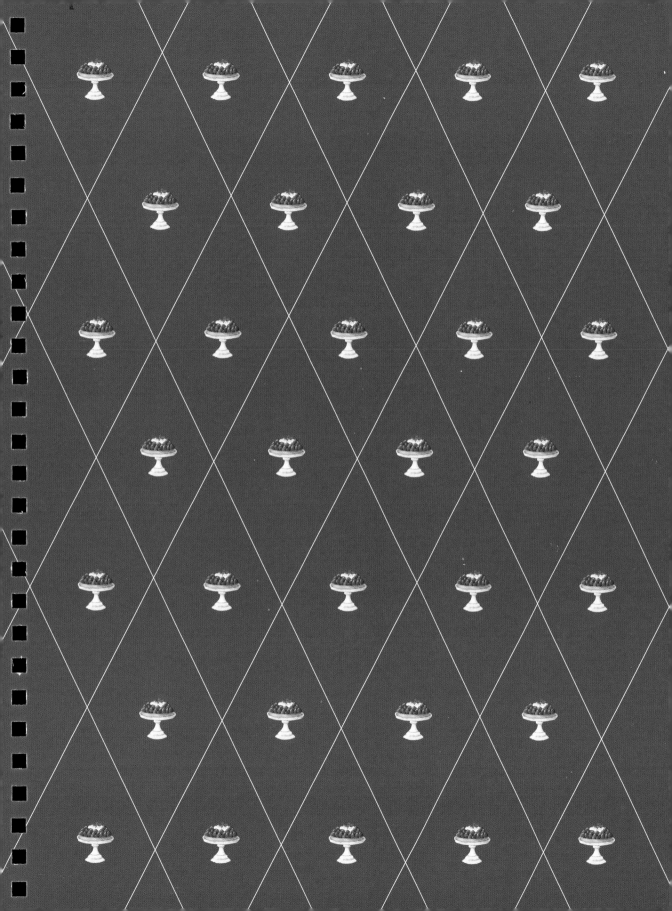

GET-TOGETHERS—
LARGE AND SMALL

*M*any occasions when we entertain do not fall under the definition of a meal per se. There are birthday parties, cocktail parties, New Year's Eve parties and Super Bowl parties. There are picnics, afternoon teas, open houses, buffets and weddings—occasions in which the foods and beverages may be served in various settings and not necessarily follow the standard sequence of courses.

Get-togethers that fall out of the rubric of a basic meal with three or four courses offer splendid and creative opportunities for entertaining. You can change the location of your event, moving from the dining table to the living room to serve tea; or outside for a picnic; or even around the television if the Super Bowl is the focal point.

A friend and neighbor, Pat, seems to have a genius for varying where her guests are going to meet. Before a get-together at her house, I find myself curious about where we will gather. When the weather is chilly, we may gather in her cozy living room overlooking a pond. In autumn, as the leaves are turning, we may start in the solarium so that we can be surrounded by the brilliant colors. In summer, we might begin an evening in her shade garden, cool and dark green, that seems to set a tone of calm serenity.

When the weather is fair, meals—buffets, picnics, weddings—can be served outside. After a few less than fortunate experiences with outside venues, I have learned to determine beforehand at what time of day the event will be and where the sun will be at that hour. We have a wonderful back porch over which is a pergola we built a few years ago. The intention is that the pergola will be covered with vines offering a shady respite under which we will be able to sip iced tea or dine. Unfortunately, in spite of my best efforts, the vines have not yet assumed the mature grandeur I await. I should have waited—and do now—to serve meals there. The pergola is attached to the west side of the house. In the morning it is shady and pleasant and the amount of shade the one fragile tendril of grapevine would render was not questioned. That was the time of day I decided it would be the perfect spot to serve lunch to a group of friends. I set the table with flowered linens and filled a white crockery jug with cool blue Cranesbill geraniums, all the while picturing the dappled shade in which we would sit. By one o'clock, however, after the guests had arrived and we were sitting down to lunch, the sun had swung in all of its August intensity over the top of the house and around the vine and roof timbers and shone directly on us. We sat there gamely, perspiring and squinting, eating a lunch that would have been perfect in the shady atmosphere I had anticipated. Had I planned more carefully, lunch would have been across the yard under the thick leaves of the locust trees. Be inventive in where you serve your guests, but know whether it will be suitable at the hour you choose—and always have a contingency plan!

You can change the containers in which you serve foods. For buffets, I often use African baskets I purchased in a museum shop for crudités, breads and flatware. Or I may serve stews in large black pottery casseroles that were made in South America. Sometimes I serve foods in copper pans and bowls. A few years ago we spent some time in the Bordeaux wine country where, at an outdoor market, I purchased a copper tart pan with iron handles. I love this pot beyond reason and find every opportunity I can to use it. Buffets offer splendid opportunities to roast vegetables in it or apple tarts or simply to fill it with red grapes.

As you go about preparing for these special events, be as inventive as you can. Instead of staying in the kitchen as you select serving pieces, roam about your house or apartment. Perhaps you have baskets tucked away in which you could serve breads or fruits. Or you could take out those dusty crystal pieces you got for wedding gifts (and which you use only when Thanksgiving is at your house) and use them outside at picnics to serve crudités and dips or chilled melon. Fill old crockery pitchers with iced tea or bread sticks. Entertaining at larger get-togethers not only gives you an opportunity to be resourceful and creative in the presentation of the meal and its visual setting, it also immediately engages your guests who sense the care, thoughtfulness and imagination that went into its preparation.

If the get-together you are having is large, advance preparation is critical—both for your comfort and your guests'.

First, do as much ahead of time as you can. If there are non-perishable ingredients you will need, buy them ahead of time. Freeze what you can so that on the day of the event as much as possible can be taken from the freezer and garnished just before you serve it.

Plan to do as little as possible at the last minute. Large events are obviously not the time to make soufflés. Choose desserts that you can make ahead and freeze. It is also the time to serve stews, daubes, tagines or whatever national mixture you prefer. Most stews get even better the day after they are cooked. Take advantage of this fact.

Keep foods simple. If you do decide to make a complicated dish, surround it with foods that are less labor intensive. For a long time, I spent inordinate amounts of time and energy preparing hors d'oeuvres only to find that many of my guests were full before they got to the main part of a buffet. Now I tend to make one special hors d'oeuvre that can be prepared ahead or offer my guests a selection of dips for crudités and address my best energies to the main part of the get-together.

Be sure that you have enough plates and flatware. A few years ago, we purchased about thirty large white plates at a discount. These are our party dishes, large enough for people to balance on their lap, plain enough to accommodate any type or design of serving dishes. We also make sure that we have enough cloth napkins, flatware, and glasses available. Again we usually buy these in quantity and almost always on sale. Given a choice, I would always prefer to use cloth napkins and real glasses. Sometimes this is simply impossible to do unless you rent them. For large groups—and particularly for casual outdoor parties—paper napkins and plastic glasses, utensils and plates might be necessary. If you do need to use them, be sure they are of high quality. Paper goods stores and kitchen suppliers have attractive paper napkins that are thick enough to feel substantial in the hand. Similarly, plastic glasses that are thick, reusable and of interesting designs are available in party and kitchen goods stores. If you do need to use paper and plastic, make sure that they are coordinated with the overall design of your party. But do keep an eye out for sales of the real thing. In the long run, they are more inexpensive and more pleasing.

Determine in advance what serving dishes you will use and what will go in each. Make sure that you know what serving utensils will accompany each dish. One woman I know, enlisting the help of her children, actually puts slips of paper in each dish noting what food will go in each. This is not a bad idea even for those of us who have no helping children readily available. In the rush of serving food for a large get-together with you as both hostess and kitchen manager, these notes clarify what goes where. They also give you ready tasks for the folks who invariably ask, "How can I help?" In a nutshell, the secrets to a successful get-together are simple:

Plan ahead

Do ahead

Be imaginative and unafraid to try something new

Relax and have fun!

Forms for these special occasions follow. They are adapted so that you can list the foods and beverages you will be serving as well as other details such as the table settings and decorative elements you have selected. Because the planning and preparation for special get-togethers may take days or even weeks, there is a space for you to develop a schedule as you prepare for it.

Get-Togethers: Large and Small

Date: _____

Time: _____

Event: _____

Guest List: _____ _____

               _____ _____

               _____ _____

               _____ _____

               _____

Food: _____

_____

_____

_____

_____

_____

Beverages: _____

_____

_____

China: _____

_____

_____

Glassware: _____

_____

Flowers, Centerpieces: _____

_____

_____

Get-Togethers: Large and Small
Schedule

Week before: _____
_____
_____
_____
_____
_____

Day before: _____
_____
_____
_____
_____

Day of Event:	task	time

Get-Togethers: Large and Small

Date: _____

Time: _____

Event: _____

Guest List: _____ _____

_____ _____

_____ _____

_____ _____

_____

Food: _____

_____

_____

_____

_____

_____

Beverages: _____

_____

_____

China: _____

_____

_____

Glassware: _____

Flowers, Centerpieces: _____

_____

_____

Get-Togethers: Large and Small
Schedule

Week before: _____
_____
_____
_____
_____
_____

Day before: _____
_____
_____
_____
_____
_____

Day of Event: task   time

Get-Togethers: Large and Small

Date: _____

Time: _____

Event: _____

Guest List: _____   _____

_____   _____

_____   _____

_____   _____

_____

Food: _____

_____

_____

_____

_____

_____

Beverages: _____

_____

_____

China: _____

_____

_____

Glassware: _____

_____

Flowers, Centerpieces: _____

_____

_____

Get-Togethers: Large and Small
Schedule

Week before: _____

_____

_____

_____

_____

_____

Day before: _____

_____

_____

_____

_____

Day of Event:	task	time

Get-Togethers: Large and Small

Date: _____

Time: _____

Event: _____

Guest List: _____   _____

_____   _____

_____   _____

_____   _____

_____

Food: _____

_____

_____

_____

_____

_____

_____

Beverages: _____

_____

_____

China: _____

_____

_____

Glassware: _____

_____

Flowers, Centerpieces: _____

_____

_____

Get-Togethers: Large and Small
Schedule

Week before: _____
_____
_____
_____
_____
_____

Day before: _____
_____
_____
_____
_____

Day of Event:	task	time

Get-Togethers: Large and Small

Date: _____

Time: _____

Event: _____

Guest List: _____ _____

_____ _____

_____ _____

_____ _____

_____ _____

Food: _____

_____

_____

_____

_____

_____

Beverages: _____

_____

_____

China: _____

_____

_____

Glassware: _____

Flowers, Centerpieces: _____

_____

_____

Get-Togethers: Large and Small

Schedule

Week before: _____
_____
_____
_____
_____
_____

Day before: _____
_____
_____
_____
_____
_____

Day of Event: task   time

_____   _____
_____   _____
_____   _____
_____   _____
_____   _____
_____   _____
_____   _____
_____   _____
_____   _____

Get-Togethers: Large and Small

Date: _____

Time: _____

Event: _____

Guest List: _____   _____

_____   _____

_____   _____

_____   _____

_____   _____

Food: _____

_____

_____

_____

_____

_____

Beverages: _____

_____

_____

China: _____

_____

_____

Glassware: _____

_____

Flowers, Centerpieces: _____

_____

_____

Get-Togethers: Large and Small
Schedule

Week before: _____

_____

_____

_____

_____

_____

Day before: _____

_____

_____

_____

_____

_____

Day of Event: task   time

_____   _____

_____   _____

_____   _____

_____   _____

_____   _____

_____   _____

_____   _____

_____   _____

_____   _____

_____   _____

Get-Togethers: Large and Small

Date: _____

Time: _____

Event: _____

Guest List: _____   _____

_____   _____

_____   _____

_____   _____

_____   _____

Food: _____

_____

_____

_____

_____

_____

Beverages: _____

_____

_____

China: _____

_____

_____

Glassware: _____

_____

Flowers, Centerpieces: _____

_____

_____

Get-Togethers: Large and Small
Schedule

Week before: _____

_____

_____

_____

_____

_____

Day before: _____

_____

_____

_____

_____

_____

Day of Event:	task	time

Get-Togethers: Large and Small

Date: _____

Time: _____

Event: _____

Guest List: _____ _____

_____ _____

_____ _____

_____ _____

_____ _____

Food: _____

_____

_____

_____

_____

_____

Beverages: _____

_____

_____

China: _____

_____

_____

Glassware: _____

_____

Flowers, Centerpieces: _____

_____

_____

Get-Togethers: Large and Small
Schedule

Week before: _____
_____
_____
_____
_____
_____

Day before: _____
_____
_____
_____
_____
_____

Day of Event:	task	time
_____	_____	_____
_____	_____	_____
_____	_____	_____
_____	_____	_____
_____	_____	_____
_____	_____	_____
_____	_____	_____
_____	_____	_____
_____	_____	_____

Get-Togethers: Large and Small

Date: _____

Time: _____

Event: _____

Guest List: _____   _____

_____   _____

_____   _____

_____   _____

_____   _____

Food: _____

_____

_____

_____

_____

_____

Beverages: _____

_____

_____

China: _____

_____

_____

Glassware: _____

_____

Flowers, Centerpieces: _____

_____

_____

Get-Togethers: Large and Small
Schedule

Week before: _____

_____

_____

_____

_____

Day before: _____

_____

_____

_____

_____

Day of Event: task   time

_____   _____

_____   _____

_____   _____

_____   _____

_____   _____

_____   _____

_____   _____

_____   _____

Get-Togethers: Large and Small

Date: _____

Time: _____

Event: _____

Guest List: _____   _____

_____   _____

_____   _____

_____   _____

_____   _____

Food: _____

_____

_____

_____

_____

_____

Beverages: _____

_____

_____

China: _____

_____

_____

Glassware: _____

_____

Flowers, Centerpieces: _____

_____

_____

Get-Togethers: Large and Small
Schedule

Week before: _____
_____
_____
_____
_____
_____

Day before: _____
_____
_____
_____
_____
_____

Day of Event: task   time
_____
_____
_____
_____
_____
_____
_____
_____
_____

Get-Togethers: Large and Small

Date: _____

Time: _____

Event: _____

Guest List: _____   _____

_____   _____

_____   _____

_____   _____

_____   _____

Food: _____

_____

_____

_____

_____

_____

Beverages: _____

_____

_____

China: _____

_____

_____

Glassware: _____

_____

Flowers, Centerpieces: _____

_____

_____

Get-Togethers: Large and Small
Schedule

Week before: _____

_____

_____

_____

_____

_____

Day before: _____

_____

_____

_____

_____

_____

Day of Event: task   time

_____   _____

_____   _____

_____   _____

_____   _____

_____   _____

_____   _____

_____   _____

_____   _____

_____   _____

GOOD FOOD—
OR,
HOW NOT TO PANIC IN THE
FACE OF UNEXPECTED GUESTS

*L*et me confess this now. I am a librarian, a fulltime card-carrying one. I know what the automatic thinking is about my profession. Librarians are supremely organized, no-nonsense left-brainers who never waste a motion. This is not always the case. Although there may be some librarians like this, I am not one of them. Personally, among the many reasons I became a librarian, one of the most salient is that my vocational choice was, I believe, a last-ditch effort to get some organization into my life.

I am also a cookbook addict. I've never met a cookbook I couldn't look at. I keep cookbooks by my bed. I read cookbooks at breakfast. From time to time I belong to cookbook clubs and once, living for a time in the north of England and unable to sleep well, I bought, for about twenty cents, a 1957 cookbook called *Plats du Jour* at a used bookstall and happily read my way to sound and dreamless sleep each night thereafter.

Given my vocation and my cookbook addiction, one would suppose that the composition of a "simple little meal"—or any meal for that matter—would be a snap for me, that drawing upon my encyclopedic cookbook reading and my librarian's training, the meals I could devise would be infinite in their variety, panoramic in their cuisines, and sparkling in their inventiveness. I only wish it were so.

But no. Faced with the thought of devising a menu, my mind travels, like a cow to its stall, to one or two tried and true formulas, leaving me a little bored before I even begin. A bored host and a bored cook are an unbeatable combination for a deadly dull meal.

It's important to figure a way out of your own particular culinary well-trodden path. Many years ago, early in our marriage, at just about the moment it dawned on me that cooking involved more than making Christmas cookies once a year, I came upon a Greek stew called *stifado*. As I remember, this stew contained beef, onions, walnuts and wine, and was served to every passing fireman—or, in our case, writer or teacher—who happened to light on our doorstep. It was, after all, a step up and away from the dish that signified our very earliest years: a tuna fish casserole made with frozen peas, canned cream of mushroom soup and, *pièce de résistance*, topped with crumbled stale potato chips. (I felt that this economical fillip was almost virtuous.) Much later, the entree of choice was a turmeric chicken breast based on a Pierre Franey recipe. This was such a popular and successful idea that it ended up on the table at the wedding of one of our sons. And, like some sort of primeval memory, it became impossible to shake when I was trying to come up with a meal. Even now, it remains the very first idea to cross my mind when planning a meal.

It's not easy to be original. My friend Catherine calls it the "white panic." She, who comes home from her busy law practice to two lively sons and a doctor-husband to then whip up a pork tenderloin with peanut sauce confesses that, in the face of company, she often can think only of serving carrot sticks. For many of us, constructing a meal that is fresh and inventive often requires some assistance.

A few years ago, faced with serving turmeric chicken one more time, I harnessed the librarian and cookbook addict to the computer and arrived at an index which I called, because the title says it all, *Good Food*.

In it, I first listed all of the cookbooks that my husband and I used regularly, as well as our own personal recipes, and gave each of them a short code name. *Lulu's Provençal Table* became "Lulu" and Pierre Franey's *Cuisine Rapide* became "CR," and so on.

Next I set up categories: "Appetizers," "Soups," "Pasta," and so forth, typing each on a separate blank sheet of paper. Then I happily and fairly haphazardly went about noting what our favorite recipes were. After not too long, I had fourteen or fifteen pages of index from which I could extract ideas that

extended our repertoire of culinary possibilities and raised the meals we prepared for others to another level of interest. I've duplicated the Good Food index in the chapter following Guests for a Meal so that you can keep both a record of meals served and a list of interesting possibilities for others.

As we go from day to day, my husband and I often find ourselves cooking wonderful foods in inventive combinations that in the life before Good Food were lost the second the cookbook closed and the meal ended. Now we try to note these meals so that we can have more ideas ready when we plan for our guests.

I want to stress here the casualness of the Good Food index. The idea is that cooking and entertaining are fun, that what is important is spending time with your friends, and that to do so, you've got to be relaxed. You can best be relaxed if your homework is done. You know you're serving a lively meal, you know when to cook what, and you've got the checklists to back you up. There's not a lot of record keeping that will ruin your spontaneity—and sometimes, at five p.m., after a day at work, that is a quality that might not abound. Write it down once and you've got it forever.

How to Use the Good Food Index

Recipe Sources

First, list the cookbooks you use in which you have favorite recipes. Next, give each of the cookbooks a code. This code will make it easier for you to use the index since you won't have to write out the full title each time. I generally use the main letters from the title for the code.

For example:
Cuisine Rapide = CR
The Mediterranean Kitchen = MK
The Way to Cook = WC

Recipes

Choose a favorite recipe to list in the index. Decide in which section it should be listed. Note it in that section. Write the code of the cookbook in which you got that recipe after it.

For example:

In Joyce Goldstein's *The Mediterranean Kitchen*, there is a recipe for Marinated Sautéed Tuna in a Fennel and Bread Crumb Crust that is utterly delicious.

I first select the category. That's "Fish." Then I note that varieties of fish are listed separately. I choose "Tuna." So I write down my recipe under "Tuna." Next I write the code of the cookbook in which it appears. The code for *The Mediterranean Kitchen* is "MK." It's as simple as that. Thus, my index now looks like this:

FISH

Salmon:_____
_____

Scallops:_____
_____

Tuna:_____
Marinated Sautéed Tuna in a Fennel and Bread Crumb Crust—*MK*

Crab:_____
_____

Mussels: _____
_____

Culling the Cookbooks

Now, you proceed through your cookbooks, adding as you go. Sometimes, I just sit down with one cookbook and index all of the recipes I use from it. More often, I add them as I cook, adding a recipe now and then as I encounter worthwhile ones. Before you know it, your index will grow and you will have a record of your favorite recipes and where to find them instantly.

For those recipes that you clip from newspapers and magazines or are given to you by friends, get yourself a three ring binder and some tab dividers. Label the dividers exactly as the Good Food Index is labeled. Tape these clipped and loose recipes into this book AND list them in your sources. For instance, in our list of recipe sources, I list all of those clipped recipes as "B," for Busch (it wasn't too hard to come up with that one!!!).

As your index grows, it will begin to look like this:

GOOD FOOD INDEX

Recipe Sources:

Busch Recipes from our ring binders=B

Cuisine Rapide=CR

How to Cook Everything=HCE

The Mediterranean Kitchen=MK

The Way to Cook=WTC

FISH

Salmon:

Crispy Skin Salmon with Gingery Greens-HCE

Salmon Steaks in Red Wine-B

Braised Whole Filet of Salmon in Wine and Aromatic Vegetables-WTC

Scallops:

Scallops Americaine-CR

Scallop and Zucchini Brochettes-CR

Scallops Sautéed with Lime-B

Tuna:

Marinated Sautéed Tuna in a Fennel and Bread Crumb Crust—MK

Tuna Nicoise-CR

Crab:

Soft-shelled Crabs with Corn and Parsley-B

Crab Cakes-HCE

Mussels:

Curried Mussels-HCE

Steamed Mussels with Chorizo and Saffron Rice-B

Good Food Index

Recipe Sources

Cookbooks and Personal Recipes: _____

_____

_____

_____

_____

_____

_____

_____

_____

_____

_____

_____

_____

_____

_____

_____

_____

_____

_____

_____

_____

_____

_____

_____

_____

_____

_____

Good Food Index

Appetizers

Good Food Index

Soups

Cold Soups: _____

_____

_____

_____

_____

_____

_____

_____

_____

_____

Hot Soups: _____

_____

_____

_____

_____

_____

_____

_____

_____

_____

_____

_____

Good Food Index
Salads

Green: _____

_____

_____

_____

_____

_____

_____

_____

_____

Vegetable: _____

_____

_____

_____

_____

_____

_____

_____

Main Course: _____

_____

_____

_____

_____

_____

_____

_____

_____

Good Food Index

Vegetables

Artichokes: _____
_____
_____
_____
_____

Asparagus: _____
_____
_____
_____
_____
_____

Beans: _____
_____
_____
_____
_____

Beets: _____
_____
_____
_____
_____

Broccoli: _____
_____
_____
_____
_____

Good Food Index

Vegetables

Brussels Sprouts:_____

_____

_____

_____

_____

_____

Cabbage: _____

_____

_____

_____

_____

_____

Carrots: _____

_____

_____

_____

_____

_____

Cauliflower: _____

_____

_____

_____

_____

_____

Chard: _____

_____

_____

_____

_____

_____

Good Food Index

Vegetables

Corn: _____

_____

_____

_____

_____

_____

Cucumbers: _____

_____

_____

_____

_____

_____

Eggplant: _____

_____

_____

_____

_____

_____

Fennel: _____

_____

_____

_____

_____

Kale: _____

_____

_____

_____

_____

Good Food Index
Vegetables

Leeks: _____
_____
_____
_____
_____
_____

Mushrooms: _____
_____
_____
_____
_____
_____
_____

Onions: _____
_____
_____
_____
_____
_____

Peas and Pea Pods: _____
_____
_____
_____
_____
_____

Peppers: _____
_____
_____
_____
_____
_____

Good Food Index
Vegetables

Potatoes: _____
_____
_____
_____
_____
_____
_____
_____

Spinach: _____
_____
_____
_____
_____

Squash: _____
_____
_____
_____
_____

Tomatoes: _____
_____
_____
_____

Turnips: _____
_____
_____

Good Food Index

Vegetables

Vegetable Melanges and Mixtures: _____

_____

_____

_____

_____

_____

_____

_____

_____

_____

_____

Other Vegetable Recipes and Notes: _____

_____

_____

_____

_____

_____

_____

_____

_____

_____

_____

_____

_____

_____

_____

_____

Good Food Index
Rice, Grains, Beans

Rice: _____
_____
_____
_____
_____
_____
_____
_____
_____

Grains: _____
_____
_____
_____
_____
_____
_____
_____

Beans: _____
_____
_____
_____
_____
_____
_____
_____
_____

Good Food Index

Pasta

Hot Dishes: _____

_____

_____

_____

_____

_____

_____

_____

Baked Dishes: _____

_____

_____

_____

_____

_____

_____

_____

Cold Dishes: _____

_____

_____

_____

_____

_____

_____

_____

Good Food Index
Main and Lunch Dishes

Tarts:_____

_____

_____

_____

_____

_____

_____

_____

_____

Sandwiches, Wraps, Pitas, Bruschetta: _____

_____

_____

_____

_____

_____

_____

_____

_____

Pizza, Calzones:_____

_____

_____

_____

_____

_____

_____

_____

_____

_____

Good Food Index

Sauces, Salsas, Seasonings and Marinades

Sauces: _____
_____
_____
_____
_____
_____
_____

Salsas: _____
_____
_____
_____
_____
_____

Seasonings: _____
_____
_____
_____
_____
_____

Marinades: _____
_____
_____
_____
_____
_____
_____

Good Food Index
Fish

Bass: _____
_____
_____
_____
_____

Cod and Salt Cod: _____
_____
_____
_____
_____

Haddock: _____
_____
_____
_____
_____

Halibut: _____
_____
_____
_____
_____

Flounder: _____
_____
_____
_____
_____

Monkfish: _____
_____
_____
_____

Good Food Index

Fish

Salmon: _____
_____
_____
_____
_____

Shad and Shad Roe: _____
_____
_____
_____
_____

Snapper: _____
_____
_____
_____
_____

Sole: _____
_____
_____
_____

Squid: _____
_____
_____
_____

Swordfish _____
_____
_____
_____
_____

Good Food Index
Fish

Trout: _____
_____
_____
_____
_____

Tuna: _____
_____
_____
_____

Other Fish (i.e. Mackerel, Mahi-Mahi, Marlin, Tilapia, etc.): _____
_____
_____
_____

ShellFish

Clams: _____
_____
_____
_____

Crab: _____
_____
_____
_____

Lobster: _____
_____
_____
_____

Good Food Index
Fish

Mussels: _____

_____

_____

Oysters: _____

_____

_____

Scallops: _____

_____

_____

_____

_____

Shrimp: _____

_____

_____

_____

_____

_____

_____

Fish Soups, Stews, Paellas: _____

_____

_____

_____

_____

Fish and Pasta: _____

_____

_____

_____

Good Food Index

Meat

Beef:_____

_____

_____

_____

_____

_____

_____

_____

_____

Veal: _____

_____

_____

_____

_____

_____

_____

_____

_____

Lamb:_____

_____

_____

_____

_____

_____

_____

_____

_____

Good Food Index
Meat

Pork: _____

_____

_____

_____

_____

_____

_____

_____

_____

_____

Sausages: _____

_____

_____

_____

_____

_____

_____

_____

_____

Game (i.e. Venison, Rabbit, etc.): _____

_____

_____

_____

_____

_____

_____

_____

_____

_____

Good Food Index
Poultry (Chicken)

Boneless Chicken Breasts: _____

_____

_____

_____

_____

_____

_____

_____

Cut-up Chicken: _____

_____

_____

_____

_____

_____

_____

_____

Whole Chicken: _____

_____

_____

_____

_____

_____

_____

_____

Good Food Index

Poultry

Game Hens: _____

_____

_____

_____

_____

_____

Turkey: _____

_____

_____

_____

_____

_____

Duck: _____

_____

_____

_____

_____

_____

Other (i.e. Capon, Goose, Pheasant, Quail): _____

_____

_____

_____

_____

_____

_____

Good Food Index

Breads

Loaves: _____

_____

_____

_____

_____

Rolls: _____

_____

_____

_____

_____

Quick Breads: _____

_____

_____

_____

_____

Biscuits and Muffins: _____

_____

_____

_____

_____

_____

_____

Sweet Breads: _____

_____

_____

Good Food Index
Desserts

Cakes: _____

_____

_____

_____

_____

_____

_____

_____

Cookies: _____

_____

_____

_____

_____

_____

_____

_____

Pies and Tarts: _____

_____

_____

_____

_____

_____

_____

_____

Good Food Index
Desserts

Frozen Desserts: _____

_____

_____

_____

_____

_____

_____

_____

_____

Fruit Desserts: _____

_____

_____

_____

_____

_____

_____

_____

Other Desserts (Creams, Mousses, Puddings, Soufflés, etc.): _____

_____

_____

_____

_____

_____

_____

_____

_____

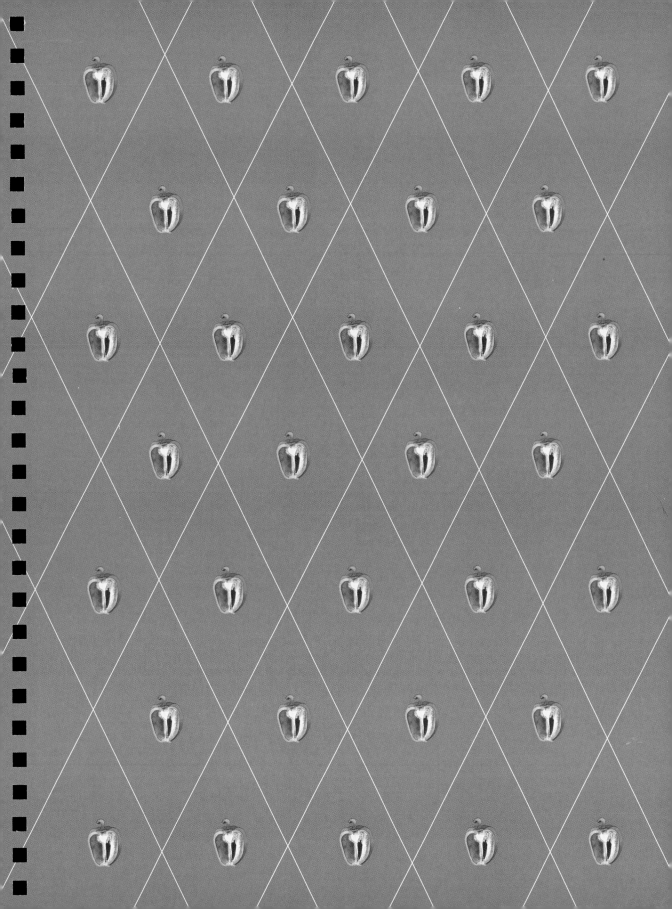

BACKGROUND MUSIC:
THE FREEZER AND THE PANTRY

Entertaining, simple or not, is easier and more comfortable if you have support systems in place. I suspect those support systems differ between city mice and country mice. If you live in a city, your support system might easily be a wonderful specialty shop where you can get tender and sweet lamb as well as the freshest of asparagus. You may have a great bakery where you can get crunchy multi-grain breads or buttery tart shells and velvety pastry cream. Making the simple little meal truly does become simpler—if costlier—and the idea of leaving your office at five and having dinner at seven-thirty not only becomes a smoother operation but a real possibility if good and interesting foods are readily available.

For those of us living farther away from the perfect French bakery, support systems are different. Three of the most critical components of my life—at least in terms of being an organized cook—are my freezer, my pantry, and the delivery truck.

The last first. My own local market has the basic staples—milk, orange juice, iceberg and Romaine lettuce, packaged cheese—and few of the tiny luxuries which make cooking and entertaining exciting and interesting. Enter that delivery truck. In this wondrous world of catalog and Internet buying, there is no reason to limit yourself to the pedestrian and not stock your freezer and pantry with delicious special foods and condiments delivered right to your door. From mail order catalogs and Internet sites come olive oil, low-fat chicken and smoked salmon sausages to be served later with French green lentils, dried mushrooms, Asian ingredients such as miso and mirin, and—the favorite of my own delivery man because his truck smells good all day—coffee beans.

A few years ago, some friends and I, in a particularly honest and refreshing moment, vowed to stop trying to decorate each other's homes at holiday gift time and instead treat each other to food delicacies we might not otherwise purchase. We are all terrifically happy about this arrangement particularly since our various freezers may hold, at any moment, smoked fish from Maine, lamb from Maryland, veal from Pennsylvania and beef from the West, all gifts and all poised for those simple little meals that are a snap and exciting to prepare with ingredients like these.

Every month or so my husband and I travel sixty-five miles to our nearest semi-large city. There, at a magnificent supermarket we buy multi-grain, sourdough, and semolina breads, polenta, bagels, boneless chicken breasts, chunks of prosciutto to add to chicken breasts with sage or to stews and sauces, and bags of frozen shrimp—cooked and uncooked. We travel to a fishmonger whose store is so clean, and the fish so fresh, that just stepping in the door is like sniffing an ocean breeze. We buy tuna, salmon and swordfish to cook in an infinite number of ways, cod and monkfish for fish soups, and scallops to grill en brochette with zucchini rounds. Upon arriving home, we wrap our bounty tightly, label it well, and store the meat and fish we are not going to use immediately in our freezer. Non-perishable items are placed on our pantry shelves. We also make sure we've entered it on our inventory of freezer or pantry foods.

Freezer Storage

After the time and expense of obtaining foods for the freezer, it's important to wrap them well so that their taste and nutritional value are preserved. We wrap meats and fish individually so that not only is defrosting time diminished but also so that we can pull out extra servings as we need them. Foods are sealed in heavyweight aluminum foil. We make sure that the foil is close to the food, therefore limiting air in the packaging. We also fold the foil several times at the points where we seal it, ensuring that the package is airtight. More often than not, we put these packages in freezer bags marking the contents, date of purchase, and place of purchase on the outside. Noting the date of purchase is important since the storage time of foods is critical. A rule of thumb is that the shorter the time foods are frozen, the more flavor and nutrition remain intact. For recommended lengths of storage times, I generally consult a reliable source such as *The Joy of Cooking*.

Candidates for the Freezer

Frequently, I cook some "background music" too. Over a weekend, I might make and freeze tart crusts, ignoring the directions for adding sugar if it's a sweet crust and simply making crusts that can be used for either sweet or savory tarts. I also make breads—focaccia, loaves of cinnamon raisin bread, baguettes and multigrain rounds that are reliable resources for guest or family meals. I use the food processor to pulse leftover bread into crumbs for topping casseroles and certain fish and meat dishes. Upon occasion, I cook lentils, beans, or wild rice and freeze them in sturdy plastic containers so that they can be called upon quickly. I make casseroles as well. I freeze in casserole dishes a family favorite—lentils cooked with a mirepoix that can be topped with chunks of meat or sausage and breadcrumbs. The original of this recipe, *Lentilles Garnies*; *Lentilles en Cassoulet*, is in one of my favorite cookbooks, *From Julia Child's Kitchen*, and is a sure-fire dish, with or without meat, served with a green salad and a good loaf of bread.

Soups and Stocks

I never resist the urge to make soup or stocks. Since I have yet to find a canned beef stock that has the ring of the real McCoy, I often buy meaty beef bones, brown them in the oven with chopped onions, celery and carrots and, once browned, bury them in a deep stock pot with more root vegetables, a tomato, salt, pepper and herbs, cover with water and let the flavors distill, bubble by bubble, for hours. Later the strained broth is frozen, sweet and delicious, and ready for stews or, on a wintry January day, Julia Child's delicious onion soup. In early spring, I pick sorrel from the garden and make soup to serve cold in the summer with a dollop of yogurt or hot in the winter. Encountering too many carrots in the refrigerator, I cook them with chicken broth and ginger for a pureed gingered carrot soup that I later top with chopped parsley and a surprising sliver of candied ginger. Each year, there comes an autumn day when the air is just beginning to bite and I entertain thoughts of hunkering down for winter when nothing will do but to make Marcella Hazen's minestrone, a veritable ballet of cooking, more fragrant it seems than any other soup in the world. In a celebration of the oncoming

COUNTRY HAM

cold weather, we always eat some of the soup then, with crusty bread and red wine, and freeze some for later in the winter when, as the soup defrosts, we are reminded of the last golds of fall, the first chill in the air.

Herbs

The herb garden—whether it's yours or your local farm market's—yields wonderful background music. I plant yards of basil, slipping some into each summer day's cooking but also making a pesto base—basil, olive oil, and pine nuts or walnuts, all pureed—which is frozen and added to soups and stews and, later with the addition of garlic and salt, put on pasta. (Garlic can turn bitter if frozen. Added fresh to the pesto base, it adds a clarity and zest.)

Some herbs should be frozen, others dried. The rafters in our barn are strung all summer long with drying bunches of herbs from our small herb garden and our vegetable garden—dill, thyme, marjoram, mint, sage, winter and summer savory, tarragon, and oregano. Once dried, we store them in glass jars for use throughout the year. We're careful to add the date on each label since their potency does diminish with age. Not all herbs are preserved well by drying. Basil, parsley, and chives are the herbal triumvirate that makes it to our freezer. Basil is laid, leaf-by-leaf, on baking sheets and frozen first

before being transferred to plastic containers. Chives and parsley are chopped and put directly into freezer containers. All winter long, we toss these by handfuls into stews and soups where they lend brightness to the darker winter flavors.

Vegetables and Vegetable-Based Sauces

Although not all vegetables freeze well, corn is one that does. During corn season, we frequently roast corn on the grill, cut it off the cob and freeze it so it can turn up some January night with shrimp or crabmeat in a soup or as an addition to polenta. Tomatoes are also strong candidates for the freezer. At the end of each tomato season, I make enough basic tomato sauce with onions, basil, and oregano to last through the winter. I make other tomato-based sauces such as Joyce Goldstein's delicious triestina sauce that is spicy and pleasantly surprising on pasta and even more delectable as the basis of a fish stew to be served over polenta. When we have a bumper tomato crop, I blanch the tomatoes so that I can remove their skins and then pack them—whole or chopped in the food processor—in pint containers.

Using the Inventory Forms

No matter what you are storing or how, it's important to keep track of it. A list or inventory of what foods and condiments are in your freezer and pantry makes cooking and entertaining infinitely easier. They permit you to see not only what is readily available but also remind you of possibilities you might have overlooked.

These inventories also can form a basis for your shopping lists as you note what you have on hand and what you need.

Not only do the freezer and pantry inventory forms which follow allow you to know what you have at any particular time, they can even spur you on to be more interesting as a cook. Although there is nothing wrong with the humble grilled hamburger, discovering that there is a duck breast in the freezer that can fit on the grill just as easily could make the difference between a ho-hum meal and one that is far livelier in conception and execution.

As we go along, we cross out the foods that we use and, every few months, we redo the inventories and start over. This procedure not only assists in entertaining: it also acts as a silent reminder to use what's been frozen or in the pantry for a while. Currently, for instance, there is a large mackerel in our freezer. I remember buying it, how silvery and fresh it looked and how it reminded me of a day long ago on a Maine beach when we grilled mackerel in the twilight. The problem is that mackerel actually seems better in that setting than baking in my oven in mid-winter. So there it sits—or lies. I remember also, with something of a shudder, opening a can of evaporated milk, which had obviously lived in the back corner of my pantry cupboard too long. Without checking the condition of the contents I added it to a carrot soup that was to be the first course of our dinner party. The anticipated smooth flow of milk did not occur, however, and I watched in horror as the milk, yellow and curdled with age, plopped acidly into my soup. There was no first course that night—at least not one with carrot soup.

Given these unsavory culinary experiences, I cannot recommend highly enough that you have a reliable reference guide to the preparing and storing of foods for the freezer and pantry on your kitchen bookshelf—and that you adhere to the suggestions in it. Many have been published. My own favorite, as mentioned before, is *The Joy of Cooking*. You might also develop a few informal methods for keeping track of foods. For instance, after the debacle of the canned milk, I now quickly mark with a permanent marker the date of purchase on all canned goods. I look forward to the time when all canned and dehydrated goods have "use by" dates on them. Until then, I'll use my trusty marker.

Keeping track of available foods and condiments is of enormous assistance as you go about organizing your cooking life. You don't have to be fanatical about it or cooking would not have the pleasure and spontaneity it deserves. The forms do give you an idea of day-to-day possibilities.

On the following pages, I've included multiple copies of both the Freezer Inventory and the Pantry Checklist so that you will be able to keep these records for many months. You may wish to make copies of the blank forms for future reference.

Freezer Inventory

Date:_____

STARTERS: _____
_____
_____
_____

SOUPS: _____
_____
_____
_____

MEATS AND FISH:
Beef:_____
_____
_____

Pork:_____
_____
_____

Lamb:_____
_____
_____

Poultry: _____
_____
_____
_____

Fish: _____
_____
_____

Sausages: _____
_____
_____

Freezer Inventory

VEGETABLES: _____
_____
_____
_____

PREPARED FOODS:

Pasta and Pasta Sauces: _____
_____

Grains and Beans: _____
_____

Savory Tarts: _____
_____

BREADS:_____
_____
_____
_____

DESSERTS: _____

Tarts:_____
_____

Cakes: _____
_____
_____

Sorbets/Ices: _____
_____

Nuts:_____
_____

Fruits: _____
_____

BEVERAGES: _____
_____
_____

Freezer Inventory

Date:_____

STARTERS: _____
_____
_____
_____

SOUPS: _____
_____
_____
_____

MEATS AND FISH:

Beef:_____
_____
_____

Pork: _____
_____
_____

Lamb:_____
_____
_____

Poultry: _____
_____
_____
_____

Fish: _____
_____
_____

Sausages: _____
_____
_____

Freezer Inventory

VEGETABLES: _____
_____
_____
_____

PREPARED FOODS:
Pasta and Pasta Sauces: _____
_____

Grains and Beans: _____
_____

Savory Tarts: _____
_____

BREADS: _____
_____
_____
_____

DESSERTS: _____
Tarts: _____
_____

Cakes: _____
_____
_____

Sorbets/Ices: _____
_____

Nuts: _____
_____

Fruits: _____
_____

BEVERAGES: _____
_____

Freezer Inventory

Date:_____

STARTERS: _____
_____
_____
_____

SOUPS: _____
_____
_____
_____

MEATS AND FISH:

Beef:_____
_____
_____

Pork: _____
_____
_____

Lamb:_____
_____
_____

Poultry: _____
_____
_____

Fish: _____
_____
_____

Sausages: _____
_____
_____

Freezer Inventory

VEGETABLES: _____
_____
_____
_____

PREPARED FOODS:
Pasta and Pasta Sauces: _____
_____

Grains and Beans: _____
_____

Savory Tarts: _____
_____

BREADS:_____
_____
_____
_____

DESSERTS: _____
Tarts:_____
_____

Cakes: _____
_____
_____

Sorbets/Ices: _____
_____

Nuts:_____
_____

Fruits: _____
_____

BEVERAGES: _____
_____
_____

Freezer Inventory

Date:_____

STARTERS: _____

_____

_____

_____

SOUPS: _____

_____

_____

_____

MEATS AND FISH:

Beef:_____

_____

_____

Pork: _____

_____

_____

Lamb:_____

_____

_____

Poultry: _____

_____

_____

_____

Fish: _____

_____

_____

Sausages: _____

_____

_____

Freezer Inventory

VEGETABLES: _____
_____
_____
_____

PREPARED FOODS:
Pasta and Pasta Sauces: _____
_____

Grains and Beans: _____
_____

Savory Tarts: _____
_____

BREADS: _____
_____
_____
_____

DESSERTS: _____
Tarts: _____
_____

Cakes: _____
_____
_____

Sorbets/Ices: _____
_____

Nuts: _____
_____

Fruits: _____
_____

BEVERAGES: _____
_____
_____

Freezer Inventory

Date:_____

STARTERS: _____
_____
_____
_____

SOUPS: _____
_____
_____
_____

MEATS AND FISH:

Beef:_____
_____
_____

Pork: _____
_____
_____

Lamb:_____
_____
_____

Poultry: _____
_____
_____

Fish: _____
_____
_____

Sausages: _____
_____
_____

Freezer Inventory

VEGETABLES: _____
_____
_____
_____

PREPARED FOODS:

Pasta and Pasta Sauces: _____
_____

Grains and Beans: _____
_____

Savory Tarts: _____
_____

BREADS: _____
_____
_____
_____

DESSERTS: _____

Tarts: _____
_____

Cakes: _____
_____
_____

Sorbets/Ices: _____
_____

Nuts: _____
_____

Fruits: _____
_____

BEVERAGES: _____
_____
_____

Freezer Inventory

Date:_____

STARTERS: _____
_____
_____
_____

SOUPS: _____
_____
_____
_____

MEATS AND FISH:

Beef:_____
_____
_____

Pork: _____
_____
_____

Lamb:_____
_____
_____

Poultry: _____
_____
_____
_____

Fish: _____
_____
_____

Sausages: _____
_____
_____

Freezer Inventory

VEGETABLES: _____
_____
_____
_____

PREPARED FOODS:

Pasta and Pasta Sauces: _____
_____

Grains and Beans: _____
_____

Savory Tarts: _____
_____

BREADS: _____
_____
_____
_____

DESSERTS: _____

Tarts: _____
_____

Cakes: _____
_____
_____

Sorbets/Ices: _____
_____

Nuts: _____
_____

Fruits: _____
_____

BEVERAGES: _____
_____
_____

Freezer Inventory

Date:_____

STARTERS: _____
_____
_____
_____

SOUPS: _____
_____
_____
_____

MEATS AND FISH:

Beef:_____
_____
_____

Pork: _____
_____
_____

Lamb:_____
_____
_____

Poultry: _____
_____
_____

Fish: _____
_____
_____

Sausages: _____
_____
_____

Freezer Inventory

VEGETABLES: _____
_____
_____
_____

PREPARED FOODS:

Pasta and Pasta Sauces: _____
_____

Grains and Beans: _____
_____

Savory Tarts: _____
_____

BREADS:_____
_____
_____
_____

DESSERTS: _____

Tarts:_____
_____

Cakes: _____
_____
_____

Sorbets/Ices: _____
_____

Nuts: _____
_____

Fruits: _____
_____

BEVERAGES: _____
_____
_____

Pantry Checklist

Date:_____

BAKING SUPPLIES:

Sugar:
❏ Granulated ❏ Light Brown/Dark Brown ❏ Confectioner's
❏ Superfine ❏ Honey

Flour:
❏ Unbleached ❏ Whole Wheat ❏ Rye ❏ Cake

Leaveners and Thickeners:
❏ Baking Soda ❏ Baking Powder ❏ Cornstarch ❏ Yeast ❏ Cream of Tartar

Syrups:
❏ Maple Syrup ❏ Corn Syrup ❏ Molasses

Flavorings:
❏ Vanilla Extract ❏ Almond Extract ❏ Orange Extract
❏ Rosewater ❏ Orange Flower Water

Chocolates:
❏ Dark ❏ Semi-sweet ❏ Unsweetened ❏ Chips

OILS:
❏ Vegetable ❏ Olive ❏ Grapeseed ❏ Peanut ❏ Walnut
❏ Light Sesame ❏ Dark Sesame

VINEGARS:
❏ Cider ❏ White Wine ❏ Red Wine ❏ Sherry ❏ Balsamic ❏ Rice

BEVERAGES:
❏ Tea ❏ Cocoa ❏ Coffee

Pantry Checklist

CANNED GOODS:

Fish:

☐ Tuna ☐ Sardines ☐ Anchovies

Vegetables:

☐ Tomatoes ☐ Tomato Paste ☐ Chestnuts ☐ Chilis ☐ Water Chestnuts

☐ Pumpkin ☐ Black Beans ☐ Kidney Beans ☐ Chickpeas ☐ Cannellini

BROTHS AND STOCKS:

☐ Chicken ☐ Beef ☐ Vegetable ☐ Clam Juice ☐ Fish Broth

CONDIMENTS:

Mustards: ☐ Whole Grain ☐ Dijon ☐ Yellow

☐ Ketchup ☐ Mayonnaise ☐ Capers ☐ Cornichons ☐ Worcestershire Sauce

☐ Hot Sauces ☐ Barbecue Sauces

☐ Soy Sauce ☐ Miso ☐ Mirin ☐ Fish Sauce ☐ Black Bean Sauce

☐ Hoisin Sauce ☐ Coconut Milk

Salts:

☐ Coarse Sea Salt ☐ Fine Sea Salt

PASTAS AND NOODLES:

Pastas:

☐ Angel Hair ☐ Couscous ☐ Fettuccine ☐ Farfalle ☐ Fuselli

☐ Lasagna ☐ Linguine ☐ Macaroni ☐ Penne ☐ Rigatoni ☐ Rotelle

☐ Spaghetti

Noodles:

☐ Rice ☐ Soba ☐ Cellophane ☐ Egg ☐ Buckwheat ☐ Somen

Pantry Checklist

RICE:

☐ White ☐ Wild ☐ Brown ☐ Rice Blends ☐ Arborio ☐ Jasmine ☐ Basmati

GRAINS:

☐ Bulgur ☐ Barley ☐ Cornmeal ☐ Oats ☐ Polenta

DRIED BEANS:

☐ Kidney ☐ Navy ☐ Black ☐ Dried Peas

☐ Lentils ☐ Soy

DRIED FRUITS:

☐ Golden Raisins ☐ Dark Raisins ☐ Currants ☐ Prunes ☐ Apricots ☐ Dates

DRIED VEGETABLES:

Mushrooms: ☐ Cepes ☐ Morels ☐ Porcini ☐ Shitake

☐ Sweet Red Pepper Flakes ☐ Chilis

JAMS, JELLIES AND PEANUT BUTTER:

☐ Strawberry Jam ☐ Raspberry Jam ☐ Orange Marmalade

☐ Apricot Jam ☐ Other jams and jellies ☐ Peanut Butter

SPICES, HERBS and SEEDS:

Herbs:

☐ Basil (best frozen) ☐ Bay leaf ☐ Celery ☐ Chervil ☐ Chives ☐ Cilantro

☐ Coriander ☐ Dill ☐ Herbes de Provence ☐ Marjoram ☐ Mint

☐ Oregano ☐ Rosemary ☐ Sage ☐ Summer Savory ☐ Tarragon

☐ Thyme ☐ Winter Savory

Pantry Checklist

Spices:

❑ Allspice ❑ Ground Cardamom ❑ Celery Salt ❑ Chili Powder ❑ Cinnamon
❑ Cloves ❑ Ground Coriander ❑ Cumin ❑ Curry Powder
❑ Garam Masala ❑ Ginger ❑ Mace ❑ Nutmeg ❑ Oriental Five Spice Powder
❑ Paprika ❑ Saffron ❑ Turmeric ❑ Zatar

Seeds:

❑ Caraway ❑ Cardamom ❑ Celery ❑ Coriander ❑ Cumin ❑ Dill
❑ Fennel ❑ Mustard ❑ Poppy ❑ Sesame ❑ Juniper

Peppers:

❑ Whole Peppercorns ❑ Cayenne Pepper ❑ Red Pepper
❑ White Pepper ❑ Ancho Chili Pepper

Pantry Checklist

Date:_____

BAKING SUPPLIES:

Sugar:
- ☐ Granulated ☐ Light Brown/Dark Brown ☐ Confectioner's
- ☐ Superfine ☐ Honey

Flour:
- ☐ Unbleached ☐ Whole Wheat ☐ Rye ☐ Cake

Leaveners and Thickeners:
- ☐ Baking Soda ☐ Baking Powder ☐ Cornstarch ☐ Yeast ☐ Cream of Tartar

Syrups:
- ☐ Maple Syrup ☐ Corn Syrup ☐ Molasses

Flavorings:
- ☐ Vanilla Extract ☐ Almond Extract ☐ Orange Extract
- ☐ Rosewater ☐ Orange Flower Water

Chocolates:
- ☐ Dark ☐ Semi-sweet ☐ Unsweetened ☐ Chips

OILS:
- ☐ Vegetable ☐ Olive ☐ Grapeseed ☐ Peanut ☐ Walnut
- ☐ Light Sesame ☐ Dark Sesame

VINEGARS:
- ☐ Cider ☐ White Wine ☐ Red Wine ☐ Sherry ☐ Balsamic ☐ Rice

BEVERAGES:
- ☐ Tea ☐ Cocoa ☐ Coffee

Pantry Checklist

CANNED GOODS:

Fish:

☐ Tuna ☐ Sardines ☐ Anchovies

Vegetables:

☐ Tomatoes ☐ Tomato Paste ☐ Chestnuts ☐ Chilis ☐ Water Chestnuts
☐ Pumpkin ☐ Black Beans ☐ Kidney Beans ☐ Chickpeas ☐ Cannellini

BROTHS AND STOCKS:

☐ Chicken ☐ Beef ☐ Vegetable ☐ Clam Juice ☐ Fish Broth

CONDIMENTS:

Mustards: ☐ Whole Grain ☐ Dijon ☐ Yellow
☐ Ketchup ☐ Mayonnaise ☐ Capers ☐ Cornichons ☐ Worcestershire Sauce
☐ Hot Sauces ☐ Barbecue Sauces
☐ Soy Sauce ☐ Miso ☐ Mirin ☐ Fish Sauce ☐ Black Bean Sauce
☐ Hoisin Sauce ☐ Coconut Milk

Salts:

☐ Coarse Sea Salt ☐ Fine Sea Salt

PASTAS AND NOODLES:

Pastas:

☐ Angel Hair ☐ Couscous ☐ Fettuccine ☐ Farfalle ☐ Fuselli
☐ Lasagna ☐ Linguine ☐ Macaroni ☐ Penne ☐ Rigatoni ☐ Rotelle
☐ Spaghetti

Noodles:

☐ Rice ☐ Soba ☐ Cellophane ☐ Egg ☐ Buckwheat ☐ Somen

Pantry Checklist

RICE:

☐ White ☐ Wild ☐ Brown ☐ Rice Blends ☐ Arborio ☐ Jasmine ☐ Basmati

GRAINS:

☐ Bulgur ☐ Barley ☐ Cornmeal ☐ Oats ☐ Polenta

DRIED BEANS:

☐ Kidney ☐ Navy ☐ Black ☐ Dried Peas

☐ Lentils ☐ Soy

DRIED FRUITS:

☐ Golden Raisins ☐ Dark Raisins ☐ Currants ☐ Prunes ☐ Apricots ☐ Dates

DRIED VEGETABLES:

Mushrooms: ☐ Cepes ☐ Morels ☐ Porcini ☐ Shitake

☐ Sweet Red Pepper Flakes ☐ Chilis

JAMS, JELLIES AND PEANUT BUTTER:

☐ Strawberry Jam ☐ Raspberry Jam ☐ Orange Marmalade

☐ Apricot Jam ☐ Other jams and jellies ☐ Peanut Butter

SPICES, HERBS and SEEDS:

Herbs:

☐ Basil (best frozen) ☐ Bay leaf ☐ Celery ☐ Chervil ☐ Chives ☐ Cilantro

☐ Coriander ☐ Dill ☐ Herbes de Provence ☐ Marjoram ☐ Mint

☐ Oregano ☐ Rosemary ☐ Sage ☐ Summer Savory ☐ Tarragon

☐ Thyme ☐ Winter Savory

Pantry Checklist

Spices:

☐ Allspice ☐ Ground Cardamom ☐ Celery Salt ☐ Chili Powder ☐ Cinnamon
☐ Cloves ☐ Ground Coriander ☐ Cumin ☐ Curry Powder
☐ Garam Masala ☐ Ginger ☐ Mace ☐ Nutmeg ☐ Oriental Five Spice Powder
☐ Paprika ☐ Saffron ☐ Turmeric ☐ Zatar

Seeds:

☐ Caraway ☐ Cardamom ☐ Celery ☐ Coriander ☐ Cumin ☐ Dill
☐ Fennel ☐ Mustard ☐ Poppy ☐ Sesame ☐ Juniper

Peppers:

☐ Whole Peppercorns ☐ Cayenne Pepper ☐ Red Pepper
☐ White Pepper ☐ Ancho Chili Pepper

Pantry Checklist

Date:_____

BAKING SUPPLIES:

Sugar:
❒ Granulated ❒ Light Brown/Dark Brown ❒ Confectioner's
❒ Superfine ❒ Honey

Flour:
❒ Unbleached ❒ Whole Wheat ❒ Rye ❒ Cake

Leaveners and Thickeners:
❒ Baking Soda ❒ Baking Powder ❒ Cornstarch ❒ Yeast ❒ Cream of Tartar

Syrups:
❒ Maple Syrup ❒ Corn Syrup ❒ Molasses

Flavorings:
❒ Vanilla Extract ❒ Almond Extract ❒ Orange Extract
❒ Rosewater ❒ Orange Flower Water

Chocolates:
❒ Dark ❒ Semi-sweet ❒ Unsweetened ❒ Chips

OILS:
❒ Vegetable ❒ Olive ❒ Grapeseed ❒ Peanut ❒ Walnut
❒ Light Sesame ❒ Dark Sesame

VINEGARS:
❒ Cider ❒ White Wine ❒ Red Wine ❒ Sherry ❒ Balsamic ❒ Rice

BEVERAGES:
❒ Tea ❒ Cocoa ❒ Coffee

Pantry Checklist

CANNED GOODS:

Fish:

❒ Tuna ❒ Sardines ❒ Anchovies

Vegetables:

❒ Tomatoes ❒ Tomato Paste ❒ Chestnuts ❒ Chilis ❒ Water Chestnuts
❒ Pumpkin ❒ Black Beans ❒ Kidney Beans ❒ Chickpeas ❒ Cannellini

BROTHS AND STOCKS:

❒ Chicken ❒ Beef ❒ Vegetable ❒ Clam Juice ❒ Fish Broth

CONDIMENTS:

Mustards: ❒ Whole Grain ❒ Dijon ❒ Yellow
❒ Ketchup ❒ Mayonnaise ❒ Capers ❒ Cornichons ❒ Worcestershire Sauce
❒ Hot Sauces ❒ Barbecue Sauces
❒ Soy Sauce ❒ Miso ❒ Mirin ❒ Fish Sauce ❒ Black Bean Sauce
❒ Hoisin Sauce ❒ Coconut Milk

Salts:

❒ Coarse Sea Salt ❒ Fine Sea Salt

PASTAS AND NOODLES:

Pastas:

❒ Angel Hair ❒ Couscous ❒ Fettuccine ❒ Farfalle ❒ Fuselli
❒ Lasagna ❒ Linguine ❒ Macaroni ❒ Penne ❒ Rigatoni ❒ Rotelle
❒ Spaghetti

Noodles:

❒ Rice ❒ Soba ❒ Cellophane ❒ Egg ❒ Buckwheat ❒ Somen

Pantry Checklist

RICE:

☐ White ☐ Wild ☐ Brown ☐ Rice Blends ☐ Arborio ☐ Jasmine ☐ Basmati

GRAINS:

☐ Bulgur ☐ Barley ☐ Cornmeal ☐ Oats ☐ Polenta

DRIED BEANS:

☐ Kidney ☐ Navy ☐ Black ☐ Dried Peas
☐ Lentils ☐ Soy

DRIED FRUITS:

☐ Golden Raisins ☐ Dark Raisins ☐ Currants ☐ Prunes ☐ Apricots ☐ Dates

DRIED VEGETABLES:

Mushrooms: ☐ Cepes ☐ Morels ☐ Porcini ☐ Shitake
☐ Sweet Red Pepper Flakes ☐ Chilis

JAMS, JELLIES AND PEANUT BUTTER:

☐ Strawberry Jam ☐ Raspberry Jam ☐ Orange Marmalade
☐ Apricot Jam ☐ Other jams and jellies ☐ Peanut Butter

SPICES, HERBS and SEEDS:

Herbs:
☐ Basil (best frozen) ☐ Bay leaf ☐ Celery ☐ Chervil ☐ Chives ☐ Cilantro
☐ Coriander ☐ Dill ☐ Herbes de Provence ☐ Marjoram ☐ Mint
☐ Oregano ☐ Rosemary ☐ Sage ☐ Summer Savory ☐ Tarragon
☐ Thyme ☐ Winter Savory

Pantry Checklist

Spices:

☐ Allspice ☐ Ground Cardamom ☐ Celery Salt ☐ Chili Powder ☐ Cinnamon
☐ Cloves ☐ Ground Coriander ☐ Cumin ☐ Curry Powder
☐ Garam Masala ☐ Ginger ☐ Mace ☐ Nutmeg ☐ Oriental Five Spice Powder
☐ Paprika ☐ Saffron ☐ Turmeric ☐ Zatar

Seeds:

☐ Caraway ☐ Cardamom ☐ Celery ☐ Coriander ☐ Cumin ☐ Dill
☐ Fennel ☐ Mustard ☐ Poppy ☐ Sesame ☐ Juniper

Peppers:

☐ Whole Peppercorns ☐ Cayenne Pepper ☐ Red Pepper
☐ White Pepper ☐ Ancho Chili Pepper

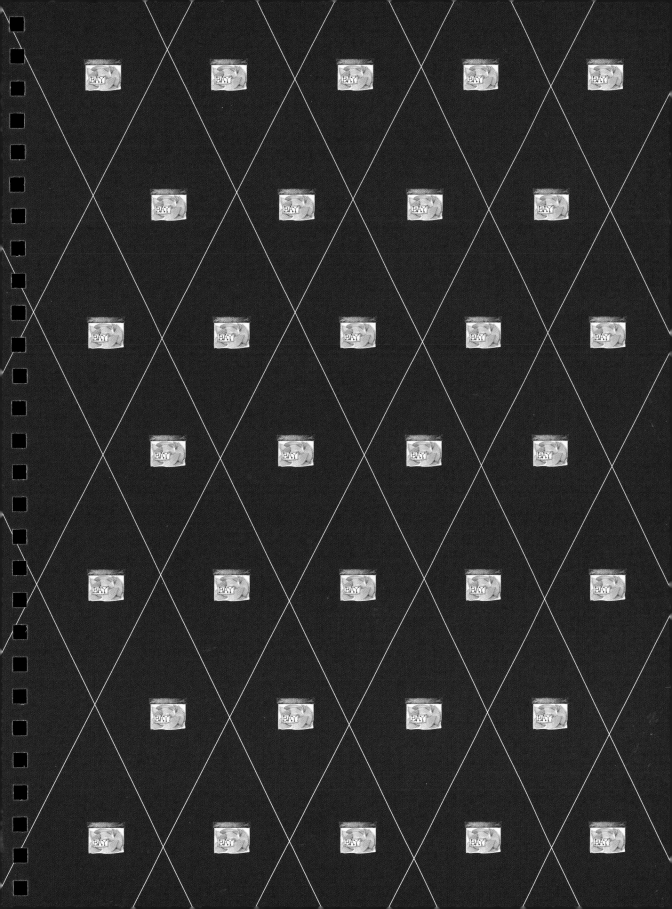

KNOW YOUR VOICE

Just as English teachers tell their students to find their own voice, so it is with cooking and entertaining. Each of us has a certain individual vocabulary consisting of the foods we like; the flavors that attract us; the dishes which go on the table; the colors of the candles; the patterns of napkins, tablecloths, and place mats; the number of objects we like to see on a surface; the objects themselves.

One of the most interesting aspects of entertaining is the setting of the scene—making decisions about the choices of colors and shapes which will establish the tone for the occasion and which, in your unique way, tells your guests that you are you. The setting of the scene should be fun, dictated by no rules except what interests you and your eye and your heart.

There is something both exciting and intimate about to going to friends' homes and sinking into their vision of the world. I have one friend whose table is always, no matter the season, set with white linen, silver candlesticks, and white candles. This may sound humdrum and terribly unimaginative, but it is not. The white and the silver have a kind of rigor, a base set of rules not unlike those that govern Japanese flower arranging. The way she plays with this white and silver austerity is continuously engaging. In the autumn, bittersweet may wind through the candlesticks. In the spring, white tulips spill voluptuously from glass vases. How she gets flowers to turn in exactly the perfect way is one of the great mysteries of life. Another friend likes clutter and her table is layered with lace and sometimes velvet; candlesticks are mismatched and high above our heads; each dish is a different and ornate pattern. Still another friend has a taste that is simultaneously modern and homespun. Plates are handmade stoneware, thick and creamy white, napkins are homespun linen, the centerpiece is a contemporary sculpture of wood and wire mesh, and the candlesticks are soaring stainless birds. Another has a penchant for porcelain figures and, as candles tower in trees of crystal candlesticks, tiny porcelain birds gather on the table below.

I love going to these friends' houses. As soon as I walk in the door, I feel comfortable and happy. Their visual "voices" are as reassuring as their real voices. The feelings are akin to opening a new book by a favorite author. One feels secure in the clarity of their vision, eager to engage in a new adventure with them, confident that what lies ahead will be wonderful.

Sometimes we don't know if we have a voice or, if we do, what it is. A few years back, a friend, describing someone I didn't know, told me how this person always used flowers just as I did. Now, strange as it seems, I really hadn't thought much about using flowers. I just knew I cut them in summer from my garden or from my back field, and, in winter, either bought them or used flowers I had dried the previous summer. But I didn't know that flowers were something people connected with me until it was mentioned.

Each of us has a singular, identifiable voice consisting of the objects we choose and how we use them. Finding that profile often entails no more than learning to listen or notice what colors and shapes we like and trusting our use of them. Knowing that there is no right or wrong, knowing that there is just your way, is important.

As a piece of music returns to its melody, each of us can return to ours. Sometimes you come up with a perfectly wonderful combination for a table. My sister Wendy once bought a quilt for a bed, laid it on her dining room table to examine it and, *voila!* she had a great cloth on which to set her Wedgwood blue dishes. She sets that table often. Once, on a hot August day, expecting a houseful of company and with a garden bereft of a flower, I gathered an armful of Queen Anne's lace from our meadow, put the flowers in a glass punch bowl, and used them as a centerpiece which seemed, in its very coolness, to cut right through the summer heat. In early spring, my Labrador Retrievers and I head for our back field, where golden marsh marigolds with glossy green leaves pop up. In squat white bowls, they beam cheerily about the season and add their good-hearted promise to our meals.

Trying to remember these happy combinations is easier if you write them down. On the following forms, jot down the combinations that work. Add to them as you can. Keep an eye out for what might appear to be anomalous to a table setting—the porcelain bird, the mesh sculpture, the scarf you picked up at a county fair, the puffs of clematis in the autumn—then dare to use them and have some fun.

My Own Voice

Table Settings to Remember

Date: _____

Event: _____

Centerpiece: _____

_____

Candlesticks/ holders and candles: _____

_____

Tablecloth, placemats and/or napkins: _____

_____

_____

Crockery/China: _____

_____

Glassware: _____

_____

Flatware: _____

_____

Serving pieces: _____

_____

_____

Notes: _____

_____

_____

_____

My Own Voice

Table Settings to Remember

Date: _____

Event: _____

Centerpiece: _____

_____

Candlesticks/ holders and candles: _____

_____

Tablecloth, placemats and/or napkins: _____

_____

_____

Crockery/China: _____

_____

Glassware:_____

_____

Flatware: _____

_____

Serving pieces: _____

_____

_____

Notes: _____

_____

_____

_____

_____

_____

_____

_____

My Own Voice
Table Settings to Remember

Date: _____

Event: _____

Centerpiece: _____

_____

Candlesticks/ holders and candles: _____

_____

Tablecloth, placemats and/or napkins: _____

_____

_____

Crockery/China: _____

_____

Glassware: _____

_____

Flatware: _____

_____

Serving pieces: _____

_____

_____

Notes: _____

_____

_____

_____

My Own Voice

Table Settings to Remember

Date: _____

Event: _____

Centerpiece: _____

_____

Candlesticks/ holders and candles: _____

_____

Tablecloth, placemats and/or napkins: _____

_____

_____

Crockery/China: _____

_____

Glassware: _____

_____

Flatware: _____

_____

Serving pieces: _____

_____

_____

Notes: _____

_____

_____

_____

_____

_____

_____

_____

My Own Voice
Table Settings to Remember

Date: _____

Event: _____

Centerpiece: _____

_____

Candlesticks/ holders and candles: _____

_____

Tablecloth, placemats and/or napkins: _____

_____

_____

Crockery/China: _____

_____

Glassware: _____

_____

Flatware: _____

_____

Serving pieces: _____

_____

_____

Notes: _____

_____

_____

_____

My Own Voice

Table Settings to Remember

Date: _____

Event: _____

Centerpiece: _____

_____

Candlesticks/ holders and candles: _____

_____

Tablecloth, placemats and/or napkins: _____

_____

_____

Crockery/China: _____

_____

Glassware: _____

_____

Flatware: _____

_____

Serving pieces: _____

_____

_____

Notes: _____

_____

_____

_____

_____

_____

_____

_____

SOME COOKBOOKS TO CONSIDER

How do we decide what cookbooks are our favorites? What determines which cookbook you will pick up most often? Is there some genetic code that sends us to one cuisine more than another? What determines what recipe will inspire us to cook better and with more flair?

In compiling the admittedly idiosyncratic list below, I've tried to distill what I look for in a cookbook. Most essential is that the recipes are reliable, producing good food every time you use them. Secondly, the recipes must be easy to follow and even the recipes that are lengthy should be written clearly and directly. Thirdly, I generally look for recipes that are interesting without being crippled by esoteric and trendy ingredients you would never have were it not for this recipe. Lastly, I want to read about the food and its context. I want to know how the author came upon this recipe or where he or she first tasted it. I want to feel as if I am sitting where the author was when this food was tasted: I want the scene set.

There are other features that seem to enhance a cookbook. Cookbooks that contain menus or recommendations for other foods to serve with a particular dish are valuable since they give a starting point when you are designing a meal. Variations on menus are also valuable. Both Joyce Goldstein and Mark Bittman (see below) use basic recipes and then provide ample variations on the theme.

Here, then, is a list of my favorite cookbooks for you to consider. At the end of this section, there is space for you to note cookbooks you may wish to use.

The Best Recipe by the editors of *Cook's Illustrated Magazine* (Boston Common Press, 1999) is an unfailingly reliable guide. If you want the definitive word on what works and what doesn't, *Cook's Illustrated Magazine* will tell you. The cooks at this magazine test and retest (one can only be overwhelmed by their patience and tenacity) until they know the absolutely most successful ingredients for any given recipe. They then make this better by providing variations on their basic "Master Recipes." These recipes are collected in this book of well over 500 pages. Whether you want to know the best way to shred cabbage, the master recipe for meat stew (beef, lamb, pork or chicken) or how to make the "Ultimate Flourless Chocolate Cake," *The Best Recipe* will tell you. Hands down, this book has the best potato salad. It is the only recipe I use.

Classic Home Desserts by Richard Sax (Houghton Mifflin, 2000) was given to me a few years ago by my sister whose desserts bring gasps of surprise and delight to her guests who cannot believe that a human being, much less one in a home and not in a fancy restaurant, has created what she is setting before them. I have no such gift and generally think that fruit and cookies are just fine, if you need dessert at all. But at dinner parties, you do need dessert. People like it; they expect it. Some even wade through the duck over which you have labored for hours just so that they can eat dessert. In his introduction, Sax describes his desserts as having "unadorned frankness." This doesn't mean that that they are without imagination. In fact, with desserts like Warm Pear Charlotte and Chef Andrea's Breakfast Polenta Cake, you find a concentration of remarkably inventive, yet unfussy, desserts. My standard pie crust comes from this book along with my daughter-in-law Tracy's favorite dessert, the most reliable Angel Food Cake recipe I've ever found. As an added bonus, Sax's recipes are absolutely foolproof and are among the few I use for guests without a trial run.

The Cook and the Gardener by Amanda Hesser (Norton, 1999) is as much a delight to read as it is a volume from which to cook. Hesser spent a year in Burgundy as a cook in a chateau. On the property where she lived and worked was a gardener, M. Milbert, whose produce provided her with cooking ingredients. Hesser follows M. Milbert and the garden through the year from spring of one year until late winter of the next. Their lives intertwining, his trust in her growing grudgingly, Hesser writes of her own increasing respect for Milbert and for the earth he so reveres. She is an elegant writer: her prose is pure and clear. But she is also a wow of a cook who really knows, as they say, her onions. The recipes are filled with detailed, but never overbearing, information about the ingredients. They follow the seasons of the year, valuing the special qualities of each. Hesser suggests other foods to serve with each recipe in the "Serving Suggestions" section of each dish. This is indeed a book for cooks—and for gardeners.

Cuisine Rapide by Pierre Franey and Bryan Miller. (Times Books, 1989 hardcover: Times Books, 2000 paperback). For many years Franey wrote a column called "The Sixty-Minute Gourmet" in the *New York Times* while Miller was the *Times* restaurant critic. My copy of this book is battered from use, the pages so used they virtually open themselves. I would not know how to make fish soup without it. The lime-marinated grilled chicken breasts are simple and quite simply delectable.

Elizabeth David Classics: Mediterranean Food, French Country Cooking, Summer Cooking (Knopf, 1985) was given to me many years ago by a famed poetry editor who loved good food as few others do. He told me then that I must make Elizabeth David's Orange and Almond Cake. It remains one of the most delectable desserts I know. Elizabeth David is more than a cook; she is an experience every cook should have. James Beard said of her, "She has the rare gift of stimulating the imagination in both mind and mouth and making you want to head straight for the kitchen." This book, along with others by her such as *Italian Food* (Penguin, 1974) and *An Omelette and A Glass of Wine* (Lyons and Burford, 1997), does exactly that. When I travel, more often than not, it is Elizabeth David who accompanies me. I know one woman who keeps a copy of *French Provincial Cooking* in a small plastic bag, so used is her copy, and so worried is she that she will lose David's recipe for roast duck. Another dear friend can recite, word for word, the introduction to David's recipe for *les daubes de boeuf*.

Essentials of Classic Italian Cooking by Marcella Hazan (Knopf, 1992) is truly the essence of her two earlier books *The Classic Italian Cookbook* (Knopf, 1976) and *More Classic Italian Cooking* (Knopf, 1978) updated and refined. A movie-making friend of mine, Italian to his core, describes life as "before Marcella" and "after Marcella" for her early books certainly drew the demarcation line between red sauce America and risotto America. In the introduction to this book as Marcella sneers at the microwave, she says, "I believe with my whole heart in the act of cooking, in its smells, in its sounds, in its observable progress on the fire." As you cook with Marcella, you will too. In this book is everything you will ever need to know about risotto. With asparagus, it is heavenly: with sausages, divine. For the organized cook, Hazen also provides menus along with guidelines for composing an Italian meal.

Home Cooking: A Writer in the Kitchen (Knopf, 1988 hardcover: HarperTrade, 2000 paperback) and **More Home Cooking: A Writer Returns to the Kitchen** (HarperCollins, 1993 hardcover: HarperCollins, 2000 paperback) by Laurie Colwin. A dear friend once gave me these and I consider that gift a turning point in my life. These two wonderful books are great to cook with but just as good to read. Colwin's essays are breezy and wise. Her approach to cooking is simple, direct and sometimes verges on the cavalier. I return to these books often. When times get tough, I start some of Laurie Colwin's Black Bean Soup and nothing seems quite as bad. If you're worried about being the perfect cook and hostess, read Laurie Colwin. Her books will make you relax. You will wish that she had been your next-door neighbor so you could have laughed together over a cup of tea.

How to Cook Everything: Simple Recipes for Great Food by Mark Bittman. (Macmillan, 1998). This is, quite simply, the first book I reach for when I'm cooking. You may think the title a little boastful: it's not. Bittman doesn't miss much in here. Better yet, his approach to cooking is inventive, flexible, and uncluttered. He frequently takes basic recipes and then gives lists of variations for them. And his taste buds are as well tuned as a fine violin. My copy has page after page spattered with his delicious food. Also take a look at his other works—*The Minimalist Cooks At Home* (Broadway Books, 2000) and *Fish: The Complete Guide to Buying and Cooking* (Macmillan, 1994 hardcover: Hungry Minds, 1999 paperback) that tells you what to do—and not do— with every kind of fish. Want to know what to do with that mahi-mahi? Bittman will tell you. He has also co-authored cookbooks with Jean-Georges Vongerichten. In *How to Cook Everything*, Bittman includes menus for regular meals and for special occasions.

The Joy of Cooking by Irma S. Rombauer and Marion Rombauer Becker (Simon and Schuster, 1997 hardcover: Penguin, 1997 paperback) is the cookbook many of us receive as wedding gifts. This is the second edition I have owned. There are several revised editions that reinterpret basic recipes based upon sound nutritional principles, provide more ethnic and vegetarian recipes, and give information about new foods that have entered the contemporary food vocabulary. Whether you need to know how to poach an egg, how to make gremolata or how long to store foods in the freezer or pantry, *The Joy of Cooking*, in any edition, is the indispensable reference. The times I have used it are countless. Faced with making a delicious birthday cake, I turn to the Four-Egg Cake that has never failed to charm child or adult. Confronting the Thanksgiving turkey carcass waiting for me in its stockpot, I check with the *Joy* to be sure I've added all I need for a tasty broth. More than a cookbook, this is a comprehensive examination of the basic information you need to know about food, cooking, and the kitchen. I couldn't cook without it.

Lulu's Provençal Table: The Exuberant Food and Wine from Domaine Tempier Vineyard by Richard Olney with a forward by Alice Waters (HarperCollins, 1994) is the essential Provençal cookbook. Olney followed Lulu Tempier for the better part of the year—the wine growers' year—and gleaned from her the recipes that appear in the book. It was no easy feat for Lulu is the apotheosis of the cuisine of the *bonne femme* and tidy measurements are not in her vocabulary. Yet the spirit of her cooking is so filled with gusto, so brimming over with the lusty flavors of the area and the text almost spellbinding in its depiction of life on the vineyard and in the kitchen, that you almost begin to believe that you are in Provence. One of my favorite recipes of all time is in here, Leg of Lamb on a Bed of Thyme. It is really quite simple. A leg of lamb, seasoned only with olive oil, salt and pepper is laid in a roasting pan on a bed of thyme surrounded by whole heads of garlic and is roasted. This recipe inspires me each summer to literally head for the hills around my house and cut bunches of thyme that I dry and store in a basket until winter when I make this dish. Then later, as I cook, there is the remembrance of the hills and cutting the thyme and of Provence. One Christmas, to one of my dearest friends in the world, I sent bunches of thyme, a leg of lamb, and this recipe. Even without cutting your own thyme, you can make this. Many supermarkets these days have a special herb section—and thyme is an herb that retains its flavor and freshness longer than most others.

Madhur Jaffrey's Indian Cooking (Barron's Educational Services, 1995) convinced me, after an overdose of it in the 60's and 70's, to rethink Indian food. Here's how. On a recent trip to old friends in the Lake District of England, jet-lagged from the flight and the drive north from Manchester, aching only for a bed, we opened the door of the restored barn they call home to be met by some mysterious fragrance, spicy, smoky and a little sweet, simultaneously. It was, my friend Lilian told me, Madhur Jaffrey's Whole Leg of Lamb in a Spicy Yogurt Sauce. I forwent the long sleep, settled for a short nap and was pulled to the table by that lamb. This is the perfect dish for *The Organized Cook*, a delicious centerpiece with spectacular flavors around which one can array any number (many or few) of dishes. Jaffrey generally suggests other dishes that can be served with her foods.

The Mediterranean Kitchen by Joyce Goldstein (William Morrow, 1989 hardcover: Morrow, 1998 paperback). In the beginning of this book, Goldstein, who owned the famed Square One restaurant in San Francisco, says that the "Mediterranean is more than a place on the map. It is a state of mind." This book is a state of mind for me, too. Goldstein's recipes are interesting and often as adventurous as Odysseus. Her *Salmone al Giuliese*—Baked Salmon with Capers and Toasted Bread Crumbs—takes minutes to prepare and the result is alchemy. An informed palate guides her son Evan's wine suggestions that comprise an extensive section at the end of this book. The suggestions are international. He is clear about types as well as specific vintages and often recommends wines that will enhance the specific flavors of his mother's recipes.

The New James Beard (Knopf, 1981 hardcover: Knopf, 1984 paperback) is just one of Beard's books we still use. Beard was in all ways in the vanguard of our national interest in good food and excellent ingredients. He was among the first to incorporate international cuisines into ours. With bows to French and Italian cooking, Beard translated daubes, stews and marinades into American cookery. He was among the first to provide variations on recipes and to include serving suggestions as well.

Patricia Wells At Home In Provence (Scribner, 1996 hardcover: Simon and Schuster 1999 paperback) is a beautiful book featuring photographs of Wells' Provençal farmhouse and the foods she cooks there. Her palate is sophisticated; she braves simplicity. She gives suggestions for accompanying dishes and wines, a service that makes life easy for the organized cook. Her Apricot-Honey-Almond Tart is every bit as easy, delectable, and beautiful as she claims. Her well-researched *Trattoria* (William Morrow, 1993 hardcover: William Morrrow, 1995 paperback) and *Bistro Cooking* (Workman, 1989) feature Italian and French dishes, most of which are easily prepared and all of which are delicious.

The Way To Cook by Julia Child (Knopf, 1989 hardcover: Knopf, 1993 paperback) is the ultimate source book. Here, the mother of a generation of cooks and the woman who single-handedly propelled American cooking out of the realm of tuna casseroles distills what she originally taught us. Although still firmly anchored in French roots, this book embraces newer ideas about nutrition without abandoning taste. The arrangement is frequently by method—for instance, the chapter on eggs includes piperades and soufflés of all kinds from lobster to chocolate. The recipes are detailed without being precious. More often than not, there is a basic recipe from which you can spring to variations. And the book retains Julia's inimitable gusto.

Weir Cooking: Recipes from the Wine Country by Joanne Weir (Time-Life: 1999) and *Joanne Weir's More Cooking in the Wine Country* (Simon and Schuster, 2001) virtually shine with the freshest of ingredients (what else do we expect of our wine country) and a bold, remarkable palate. I refer to these books when I want to turn the interest up a notch. For instance, if you plan on having salmon, how about in early spring with asparagus and blood oranges or in winter as Crisp Salmon with Green Herb and Caper sauce? Weir's vision of food and cooking is utterly clear: there are no muddy flavors here. There is, almost always, an unexpected piquance and the irresistible bounty of California. As a bonus for those of us who like to know what the food will look like once we cook it, each book has superb and enticing photographs directly accompanying the text.

More Cookbooks to Consider